HANNIBAL'S INVISIBLES

HANNIBAL'S INVISIBLES

G. FAYE DANT

Belt Publishing

Publication of this volume was assisted by Art of the Rural through a grant from the Chicago Community Foundation.

Copyright © 2024, G. Faye Dant
All rights reserved. This book or any portion thereof may not be reproduced or used in any manner whatsoever without the express written permission of the publisher except for the use of brief quotations in a book review.

First Edition 2024
ISBN: 978-1-953368-76-8

Belt Publishing
5322 Fleet Avenue, Cleveland, OH 44105
www.beltpublishing.com

Book design by Jordan Koluch
Cover by David Wilson

Table of Contents

Dedication	vii
Acknowledgments	xi
Foreword	xiii
Introduction by Shelley Fisher Fishkin	xxiii
Chapter 1: EARLY HANNIBAL	1
Chapter 2: WATER, WATER EVERYWHERE	11
Chapter 3: A COMMUNITY WITHIN	29
Chapter 4: FRIENDS, FAMILY, NEIGHBORS	67
Chapter 5: LEARNING AGAINST ALL ODDS	99
Chapter 6: LET GO AND LET GOD	123
Chapter 7: ALL GAVE SOME, SOME GAVE ALL	139
Chapter 8: ORGANIZING FOR CHANGE	157
Chapter 9: WE SUNG! WE DANCED! WE LOVED!	173
Chapter 10: RUN, JUMP, DRIBBLE, THROW	189
Chapter 11: INTEGRATION HAPPENS	195

Dedication

Arnetta Green Stamps Sanders Smith (1921-2008). As you can see, she is beautiful! She was also smart, hard-loving, and God-fearing.

Hannibal's Invisibles is dedicated to Arnetta Green Stamps Sanders Smith, my mother. Arnetta was born on November 22, 1921, in Eolia, Missouri, about forty-five miles southeast of Hannibal. She was the oldest child of Earl and Geneva Walker Green, who had nine children—three boys and six girls: Earl, James, Wilburt, Mendill, Genevieve, Mary Ella, Edna Mae, and Mayna. Everyone referred to Mom and my aunties as "the Green Girls." They were all good-looking women and had beautiful figures.

Mom married her first husband, Charles E. Stamps, in 1940. Their first son, Charles Jr., was born in 1941 and was just fifteen months old when he died of pneumonia. Their second son, Richard, was born in 1942 and died in 2006. Mom and Charles were divorced, and my older brother Richard was raised with me and my three other brothers. Richard was fiercely protective of me and cherished his family. He also loved music—he was a drummer and traveled all over with an awesome local band. Thinking back on it, our house was probably one of the loudest on the block—he was always practicing! I can still see that big, glittery, red, acoustic drum set filling up half the living room.

I ended up with two older brothers (Richard and Mike) and two younger ones (Larry and Ronnie). We had three stepfathers: George Hayden and Virgil Sanders were the men who raised us. Mom was also a surrogate mother to several foster children. I credit her with teaching us patience and tolerance, as some of these children had some pretty severe disabilities.

She was a fierce defender of all her children. Larry tells the story of an event that occurred at Pettibone School soon after integration, when a white teacher slapped him across the face: "I took off for home, about half a mile. Mom saw my tears, turned off the burner, adjusted her headscarf, and escorted me back to school. She bypassed the principal's office and marched into my classroom. By the time she finished, the teacher was begging her to please leave, and promising to never again slap a Douglasville child."

"If my kids need a whipping," she'd say, "I'll be the one to do the whipping." Like I said, hard-loving.

Us kids lived all over. Me and my family lived in Michigan, Minnesota, and Illinois. Richard landed in Illinois, Larry in North Carolina, and Ron in Nebraska. Mike, a scoundrel and everyone's favorite, lived all over the country but ended up in Hannibal, where he married his fifth wife, AnnaLee Woodson. Mike died young; he was born in 1946 and died in 2000. Mom was proud of the fact that "he had one of the biggest funerals in Hannibal." Friends and family came from near and far, including the five wives, six daughters, and one son to mourn his passing. I said Mike was a scoundrel, but I'm being nice. He was a criminal. Everyone in the family has a story about Mike. He once told me, "I'm not a thief because I steal, I steal because I'm a thief." Mike was funny, smart, and generous. Our cousin Tyrone likes to tell about the time Mike loaned him a brand-new cherry-red Cadillac—as a University of Missouri student and recipient of a Pell grant, it was very uplifting to cruise around campus in such a beautiful vehicle. Tyrone learned later that it was stolen, and he had been stashing it for Mike. But since this is about Mom: if Mike was imprisoned anywhere close to home, Mom would take us to visit him—and of course, he assured us that it was the last time.

I think of Mom as a survivor. In the early fifties, in response to the housing shortage, the federal government and the city of Hannibal built some subsidized housing. Units for Negroes were located on Rock Street in Douglasville. They were meant for World War II veterans and their families, and even though my mom was not a vet or married to one at the time, she somehow got us into one of those brand-spanking-new apartments. At the time, she was listed in the 1955 City Directory as Mrs. Arnetta Green. Like I said, a survivor!

We may have been poor, but she sure knew how to keep us fed. She came from a family of hunters and foragers. A great cook, known for her ability to roast a raccoon, fry a carp, catfish, or buffalo fish—even a rabbit or squirrel. I can still see the grease can sitting on the kitchen stove. "Green hunting"—or "foraging" (as it's called today)—for a mess of wild greens is something she taught all of us how to do as we walked our Douglasville neighborhood. "Don't pick anything too close to the road," she'd warn as we combed the weeds for dandelions, crow's feet, or lamb's quarter. She moved to the Westside later in life and then depended on Freddy LaJoy to provide the greens, the raccoons, and the buffalo fish.

She could never convince my son, Joel Jr., to try her Thanksgiving chitlins. However, my daughter Jenni recalls "licking Grandma's mashed potato pot clean." Kalecia, another one of our daughters and an excellent cook herself, will carry Mom's mac and cheese recipe to her grave.

Late in life, Mom became an honest-to-goodness church lady. She was ultimately responsible for the kitchen at Eighth and Center Streets Missionary Baptist Church, which was our family church for generations. This was not surprising, as I remember her working most of her life as a domestic and cook for white families and restaurants all over town. As the years passed, her siblings and children moved on, but she held down the homeplace in Hannibal. She kept herself very busy and adopted many locals to replace absentee loved ones. I recently learned that she was listed as an employee for the neighborhood day care center, Della's Day Care—rocking babies to sleep was one of her gifts. She began scrapbooking, and of course, she clipped everything even remotely related to the Black community—that is, anything the local white newspaper, the *Hannibal Courier-Post*, found to be worthy of publishing. I credit her for giving me my sense of pride in community and family as well as my passion for history. She also had a great sense of humor and was fun to be around; able to turn any gathering into a party; people couldn't help but laugh at her quick wit. I don't recall her being much of a joiner, but I found her name on the membership roster of the Fannie Griffin Arts Club, a Negro women's organization committed to supporting local youth by hosting events and raising money for scholarships.

As she aged, she had to give up her independence, living with each of us for a period—first in Lincoln, then in Fayetteville, then in Rockford, and finally in suburban Chicago, where she died in our home. When she passed at age eighty-seven in 2008, she had a slew of grandchildren, great-grandchildren, and great-great-grandchildren. Three husbands had preceded her in death. Her final wishes included a "big" Hannibal funeral and to be cremated, with the ashes shared by her children and grandchildren. None of us wanted a traditional urn. I purchased lovely perfume bottles and filled each of them with ashes, and they are now proudly displayed in our homes. This way, Mom would always be where the action was. She didn't want to miss anything.

Acknowledgments

Thanks to all who provided encouragement and resources to complete this book, and thanks for the rescued photographs that are included in this book. Specifically: Hannibal Free Public Library, Arnetta Green Stamps Sanders Smith, Donald and the late Betty Forte Scott, Joe Miller, Estel and Major Griggsby, Choteau Simon, Janet Howard, Marsha Mayfield, Tommy Weathers, Angela Griffin, Rosa Ford Taylor, and Jimmy Ford.

We also acknowledge local former and current residents who contributed to the dialogue by taking time to reminisce on these long-gone people and places. It's community historians like these who added so much to the narrative: Specifically:

Alicia Williams
Valarie Hawkins Shaw
Joel Dant
Melvin Dant
Billy Morrison
Larry Thompson
Brenda Thompson
Patricia Blackwell Snoddy
Valarie Mosely
Sonny Fitzpatrick
Lilly Divers King Jackson
Patricia Smith Ford
Robert "Bob" Frazier
Marjorie Frazier

Hope I haven't forgotten anyone. If I have, forgive me.

Foreword

Alicia Jones Williams and I share a birthday. She claims to be younger than I am. To this, I nod and smile. The truth is unknown; neither of our mothers could recall.

Alicia was raised and has lived in Hannibal most of her life. She now lives in the historic Mark Twain Hotel, which was converted into a senior living facility in 2006. I'm envious; her living room has a view overlooking the Mississippi River.

Alicia is a community historian, and when I asked if I could interview her for this book, she readily agreed. On a Tuesday in October of 2021, I showed up at her home with tacos from a local bar (no margaritas, as she's on medication). On our earlier visits, we'd usually been surrounded by three generations—most often her daughter Felecia (who we call Fish), her granddaughter Anjelicia (who we call Sissy), and Sissy's five children, ages one through eleven. Like her, they've all grown up here in Hannibal. The apartment was empty and quiet the day of my visit.

The Westside, where most homes have now fallen into disrepair and many have been demolished, leaving behind weedy empty lots like what you see here. This photo was taken by Angela Griffin, from her mother Fannie Griffin's back porch.

Benjamin Howard, "Mr. Bennie," was born in Shelbyville, Missouri, in 1893 to formerly enslaved parents. He was a small man, not more than five feet tall, and somewhat eccentric.

I brought some photographs with me, and like always, Alicia and I got to talking, laughing, reminiscing, and, yes, gossiping. Alicia is incredible, and she could tell me who was who, where they lived, who married who, and all about the children they had (whether they were supposed to or not).

"That's Aunt Edna," she said, for example, pointing to one photo, "she was lovely, and she taught me how to take care of my body. As a kid, I stayed with her and Uncle Raymond Brown as often as I could. I was devastated when they moved to Virginia." Rev. Brown had received an offer he couldn't refuse. He had proven himself to be quite enterprising, having convinced Second Christian Church to purchase the venerable old Douglass School when it closed its doors in 1958. For more than eighty years, Douglass had educated generations of Black students before Hannibal integrated its public schools.

Looking at another photograph, she said, "That's Mr. Bennie. He was a character, always wore that derby hat on the side of his head. I remember that whenever he was seen walking, if asked if he wanted a ride. He'd reply, 'No'm, I'm in a hurry.'" We laughed long and hard at that. He worked as a laborer and a dishwasher. We don't think he ever married and believe he lived down on Settles Street when he died.

Alicia looked at another photograph and continued: "That's "Miss Lucille." She worked at Kresge, at the corner of Broadway and Main. "Me and my friends would go downtown every Saturday for a Kresge tuna sandwich. Against the rules, Miss Lucille would point out several stools at the end of the counter, next to the kitchen. We quickly ate our sandwiches and left, not wanting her or us to get in trouble." Even these small acts of defiance showed how Miss Lucille was a community leader who got things done. She was a loving wife, mother, and a lifelong Hannibal resident. Married to William Morrison Sr., Miss Lucille spent some years with Kresge before moving on to Levering Hospital as an EKG technician. Retired, she was sought after for many local board positions, including a charter board member for Douglass Community Services. Miss Lucille was a dedicated member of Willow Street Christian Church, where her daughter Minnie became pastor.

"Mr. Thomas Miller," Alicia continued, looking at another photograph, "he was a Douglass School teacher and a neighbor, one of the most handsome men I had ever seen." She and I then spent the next thirty minutes debating who Hannibal's best-looking man was.

Alicia is a true "community historian." But aren't we all? Because when the stories of a long-gone African American community like the one in Hannibal were never recorded and have all but disappeared, talking, laughing, reminiscing, and gossiping often give us the oral history of the town. In these memories, we hold Hannibal's past. The story of this community is interwoven with all our struggles and hurdles, as well as our accomplishments and achievements.

Lucille Moore Morrison (1919-2003). She carried herself with the dignity you see in this photograph.

Many of the photos in *Hannibal's Invisibles* were taken by Black Hannibalians themselves and are part of the growing collection at Jim's Journey: The Huck Finn Freedom Center.

Our parents and grandparents were either enslaved or lived under Jim Crow and struggled with survival for decades, both before and during the civil rights movement. Though Hannibal had no signs indicating "Colored" and "White Only" establishments and services, segregation was very real in employment, education, the restaurants, and even the hospitals. I contend that segregation without signs—where generations were quietly taught to "know our place"—was even worse and even more insidious.

In these years, like much of the country, many of us migrated in droves to larger, safer, friendlier communities with more job opportunities—places like St. Louis, Kansas City, Chicago, even Gary, Indiana.

This phenomenon continues today, as our best and brightest are encouraged to "escape" Hannibal. But those of us who chose to stay or to return struggle to tear down the walls hampering us, and to uplift those before us—our icons.

Hannibal's Invisibles is here to introduce and formalize the lost Black narrative of this rural Missouri community on the Mississippi River. With these photographs, my goal is to reclaim this space with the evidence of our existence. Stories and photographs can be a powerful force for social change. These vintage photos and firsthand accounts of Hannibal's earliest people and places will give you a glimpse of the way these men, women, and children lived, learned, worked, and played. With that visibility comes worth, and with that worth comes humanity.

TELLING OUR OWN STORY

I am very proud to be a voice of local African American history and culture in Hannibal. I'm a firm believer that we must own and tell our own stories—after all, the pain and the happiness was ours. While I don't propose to be the sole historical authority here, I have committed several

Many of the photos that find their way to Jim's Journey are images of people whose names have been lost to time.

Mary Lou Nearing Simon (1921–1983), a Douglass School graduate.

years to researching and preserving this history with accuracy and integrity. There will inevitably be mistakes—a misspelled name or a misidentified person, address, or date. But this is true of the challenges many Black people face in trying to recapture and preserve our history.

In 2011, when I first started to receive photographs from various sources, I could see the story of our people unfolding. I could see faces and places I knew and loved as a kid come alive—there was a story to tell. I founded the Hannibal African American Life and History Project, and created an exhibit in our Hannibal History Museum. It was a small room plastered with Black faces—and I saw tourists walk in, turn around, and leave. I began to recognize that most tourists who came to Hannibal wanted to get some kind of connection to Mark Twain, and they didn't think Black people had anything to do with him. In 2013, I acquired a little building downtown and relaunched as Jim's Journey: The Huck Finn Freedom Center, and donations began to pour in.

In the spring of 2014, a man showed up at Jim's Journey with a scrapbook that had been created by long-gone Hiawatha Crow; he had purchased it at a yard sale. It's best described as the Eighth and Center Streets Missionary Baptist Church history. I gave it to them; Mrs. Crow must have intended them to have it. Another time, my friend Tommy Weathers showed up at the museum with a half dozen photo albums he had found in an abandoned home that he had been hired to tear down. He recognized the value of these photographs to the narrative of the Black community and donated them to the museum, along with some vintage toys and other Jim Crow memorabilia. My husband's cousin, Major Griggsby (1928–2020), generously donated some photographs and all of his Douglass School yearbooks. Major died in 2020, and I attribute his death to COVID. He committed every Sunday afternoon to Jim's Journey and was our one and only docent. He loved our community and took great pleasure in sharing our stories. His children—Monique, Paul, Tenya, Demetrius, Nicolette, and Marquestria—also donated more memorabilia from the estates of both their father and their uncle, Estel Griggsby (1912–2017). The list of items and the people who donated goes on and on. Everything donated has been invaluable in telling who we were and the lives we have lived.

Rigorous historical research is the foundation of *Hannibal's Invisibles*. It is learned from birth and death certificates, obituaries, directories, newspaper clippings, and even Mom's forty-year-old scrapbooks.

The stories included here are rooted in the places that have molded us—they are the ingredients that shape our lives in Hannibal now. And when these communities were lost, something intangible and irreplaceable was destroyed. Here, in *Hannibal's Invisibles*, the stories of Colored places and Colored faces have been resurrected. This collection of vintage photographs and narratives will give you a sense of what life was like in our African American community along the banks of the Mississippi in northeastern Missouri.

Hannibal's Invisibles is more than a book. It is an invitation to know us as we truly were. As Congressman John Lewis, a standard-bearer of the civil rights movement and of equity in this country, said, "The movement without storytelling, is like birds without wings."

Introduction

by Shelley Fisher Fishkin

Faye Dant, the author of *Hannibal's Invisibles*, tells us that, for many years, the only official reference to African Americans in Hannibal, Missouri, was a racist sign that greeted visitors from all over the country. It read, "Here Huckleberry Finn and Niggar Jim [*sic*] stopped for a few days on their way down the Mississippi."

Dant knew that Hannibal's Black history—from slavery to the present—was complicated and rich and deserved to be documented. After spending years collecting materials that bore witness to this history, in 2013, she opened Jim's Journey: The Huck Finn Freedom Center, "to reclaim our story." For the last decade, Jim's Journey, the only Black history museum in northeast Missouri, has been an illuminating stop for visitors. *Hannibal's Invisibles* now makes that history accessible to a broader public.

In the early 1900s, the offices of the first Black newspaper published in Hannibal—a weekly called the *Home Protective Record*—burned in a fire, ending its short run less than a year after it began publication. There has been no written record of the world in which Hannibal's Black residents struggled to raise their families and build their lives in a community that was glad to have them launder their clothes, cook their dinners, and mop the floors of their municipal buildings, but didn't expect them to ever do anything much beyond these circumscribed tasks. Until now.

The story of Hannibal's Black residents was not a story that "America's Hometown" had much of an interest in preserving. "America's Hometown" celebrated *Tom Sawyer* and whitewashed fences but ignored the Mark Twain who was a critic of racism—including the racism of his hometown—and erased most physical traces that remained of the Black community that had lived in Hannibal continuously from the time of slavery to the present, a community that shaped Mark Twain's work in indelible ways.

Hannibal's economy revolves around a writer who created one of the first fully drawn Black fathers in American fiction, a character based in part on enslaved people he knew during his childhood, such as Daniel Quarles, a father himself and a gifted storyteller whose history features prominently at Jim's Journey and in this book. Mark Twain learned much of his art by listening appreciatively to Quarles's stories, as well as to the satirical sermons preached daily by an enslaved man named Jerry, whom he viewed as "the greatest man in the country." Although Twain's earliest writings against racism focused on the hostility and discrimination that the Chinese faced in the American West, he would soon come to view the slaveholding world of Hannibal in which he had grown up as morally bankrupt. He would recognize the community's largely unquestioning acceptance of a shockingly unjust status quo as a prime example of what he would call "the lie of silent assertion." "It would not be possible for a humane and intelligent person to invent a rational excuse for slavery," he wrote. Yet opponents of slavery "could not break the universal stillness that reigned, from pulpit and press all the way down to the bottom of society—the clammy stillness created and maintained by the lie of silent assertion—the silent assertion that there wasn't anything going on in which humane and intelligent people were interested."

Twain would make the racism he encountered here central to one of the greatest works of American literature, *Adventures of Huckleberry Finn*, as well as many other works. For the rest of his life, Twain continued to bear witness to the ways in which racism undermined many nations' claims to being "civilized." "There are many humorous things in the world," he wrote in *Following the Equator*, "among them, the white man's notion that he is less savage than the other savages."

Hannibal's Invisibles offers a moving record of individuals who lived their lives under the long shadow of slavery and Jim Crow, who were constrained but not crushed by the racism they had to negotiate on a daily basis; of people who, in the face of daunting odds, established a supportive community that helped its members survive and, in many cases, thrive. The many photographs that Dant has collected from various local sources help bring the stories of this community alive.

Enslaved Black people brought here from Kentucky, Virginia, Tennessee, or the Carolinas cleared the land and built Hannibal's houses and roads. They were also skilled tailors, seamstresses, horsemen, barbers, cooks, carpenters, brickmasons, nurses, cooks, maids, and butlers who made it possible for the town to grow and prosper. "Even though enslaved people had built Hannibal from the ground up," Dant tells us, "as a community, they were kept from reaping the benefits of their labor. So, their descendants built a second

Hannibal, and with it, they provided us with a future." This book tells the story of that "second Hannibal."

It's the story of a child named Emma Knight, who saw her father put up on the auction block because her Hannibal master wanted to buy something for the house—and it's the story of children who went to work, after slavery ended, on the very farms where their parents and grandparents had been enslaved.

It's the story of dozens of runaways who served in Black regiments in the Union Army. And it's the story of two brothers who served in the only African American infantry division to see combat in Europe during World War II, only to find that the GI Bill's promise of educational training turned out to be for "whites only" in their hometown: only after Hannibal schools integrated in 1955 would these Black veterans be admitted to a vocational training school for automotive repair run by the Hannibal public school system that had rejected them earlier.

It's the story of close-knit families and supportive friends—of neighbors helping neighbors in "the Bottoms" when Bear Creek periodically flooded, depositing knee-high mud over everything in sight. "The Bottoms," in Hannibal's Fifth Ward, was some of the least desirable land in town, but it was one of the few areas where Black residents were allowed to build or purchase homes. Families like that of Valerie Hawkins Shaw recall the vibrant community that residents built in this soggy floodplain, knowing instinctively to open the front and back doors of their houses to let the water flow through, leaving everything covered with mud but the house still standing. Everyone pitched in when it was time for the "horrendous cleanup process" that followed.

It's the story of students who learned to read at the segregated Douglass School. There was Fannie Griffin, who later trained at the respected Homer G. Phillips Hospital in St. Louis, only to find that "Black nurses were not welcome in Hannibal hospitals." There was Donald L. Scott, who went on to become CEO of the Library of Congress. And there was John Roland Redd, who donned a turban, took the name Korla Pandit, passed as South Asian, and became a nationally known musician. Other Douglass School graduates became attorneys, doctors, entrepreneurs, authors, scientists, and ministers. Douglass students had to make do with hand-me-down textbooks from the white school—but a revered history teacher, Marion Powers, taught them Black history "out of his hip pocket."

It's the story of a student named Joel Dant (Faye Dant's husband) and his brother, the first Black students in a rural one-room schoolhouse near their Hannibal family farm. Joel and his brother, great-grandsons of an enslaved man named Henry Dant, who was born the same year Sam Clemens was born, arrived at school one day "to find a rifle placed across their teacher's desk. On the blackboard were the crudely written words, 'KILL ALL

NIGGERS.'" After he told his father about the incident, his father took to carrying a gun to all school gatherings.

It's the story of Joel Dant's aunt, Lydia Doolin, who had to wait to start cooking the elaborate Christmas feasts she prepared for her family (the menu—included in the book—is mouth-watering) until she had finished cooking and serving Christmas dinner to her white employers. "It's easy to get angry," Dant writes, "when thinking about how exhausted our women must have been on the days they should have been enjoying their families. But they still took the time to feed us an unforgettable spread. That's love, and that makes the memories of those sweet potato pies just a little bit sweeter."

It's the story of people who had to endure endless small and large humiliations and insults—like the father who, when asked by his child why he allowed white people to call him "son and boy," responded, "I do this so we can eat." But it is also the story of people who lived, learned, worked, and played in spite of those humiliations and insults, who created self-contained neighborhoods to which they could retreat with dignity and without fear.

It's the story of children who sang in choruses and choirs, put on plays, and played in the best band in the state. Children who put on talent shows, played sports, and were Boy Scouts and Girl Scouts. The story of children who earned pocket money by babysitting, shoveling snow, cutting grass, collecting soda pop bottles, selling homemade potholders, and hawking earthworms to local fishermen. Children who would go to one of the local Black lodges for donated school supplies or to secure a reference letter for a job.

It's the story of parents employed by the town's white families as domestics, laundresses, yardmen, janitors, and chauffeurs, who managed to care for their own children with devotion and determination, advocate for them, and help guide them, against all odds, to careers in medicine, law, education, business, and other fields.

The blend of vintage photographs, firsthand accounts, and historical research brings these stories alive, celebrating what individuals in that community achieved while never losing sight of the obstacles they had to overcome in the process. Much as Black newspapers in the nineteenth and twentieth centuries had to strike a careful balance between positive stories celebrating what Black Americans were achieving and negative stories reminding readers of the discrimination, violence, and injustice against which they continually had to fight, *Hannibal's Invisibles* manages to convey the vibrancy and the joy Black residents experienced in this caring, close community while reminding us (through not only personal reminiscences but also the insertion of references to broader historical contexts and captions that speak worlds) how their white fellow citizens tried to make the canvas on which they could paint their lives as small as possible.

For example, there is a snapshot from the sixties of Louis and Margaret Dixon standing proudly in front of the restaurant they owned, a place where Black teenagers liked to hang out. "The Cafe" was especially appreciated, since Black residents were not welcome at other local eateries. It was a place where they did not have to experience second-class status—unlike the skating rink, where they could skate only on "Negro Skate Nite," and where they couldn't rent skates as white teenagers could: they had to bring their own.

There's a 1955 photo of Hannibal High's first integrated basketball team, which included three Black players. One of them, Joe Miller, was on the starting lineup. He recalled, "the coach told us that he would have started all three Blacks if he was not afraid of community backlash." Miller would later serve as the only Black member of the Hannibal Board of Education, until recent years.

There are photos of a 1968 protest against segregationist George Wallace, who was invited by the KKK to speak in Hannibal as part of his presidential campaign. Black students—including one who grew up to write this book—clergy, residents, and community leaders ran him out of town that day. The parade that had been scheduled for the next day had to be canceled.

There are images of ordinary life frozen in time—a 1955 photo of the last graduating class from the segregated Douglass School; a 1957 photo of a little child unhappy about getting his first haircut at a local barbershop; and others from that same year of some adolescent boys running a footrace and of a handsome local doctor paying a house call. There's a 1950s photo of adorable children in their Sunday best, and another of two local schoolteachers on vacation at Pikes Peak.

There's a 1993 photo of an election ad urging readers to reelect Hiawatha M. Crow to the Third Ward City Council: "She wants Hannibal to be Prosperous and Progressive," it read. When she won her first election, becoming the first Black woman elected to local office in Hannibal, the event was so noteworthy it was featured in *Jet* magazine.

Hannibal's Invisibles offers glimpses into the lives of the children, grandchildren, and great-grandchildren of the enslaved people who built the town, kept it running, and inspired the world-famous writer who grew up here. It documents the racism they endured and the resilience and strength with which they countered forces arrayed to limit what they could do and what they could dream. It is a story that Americans need to hear.

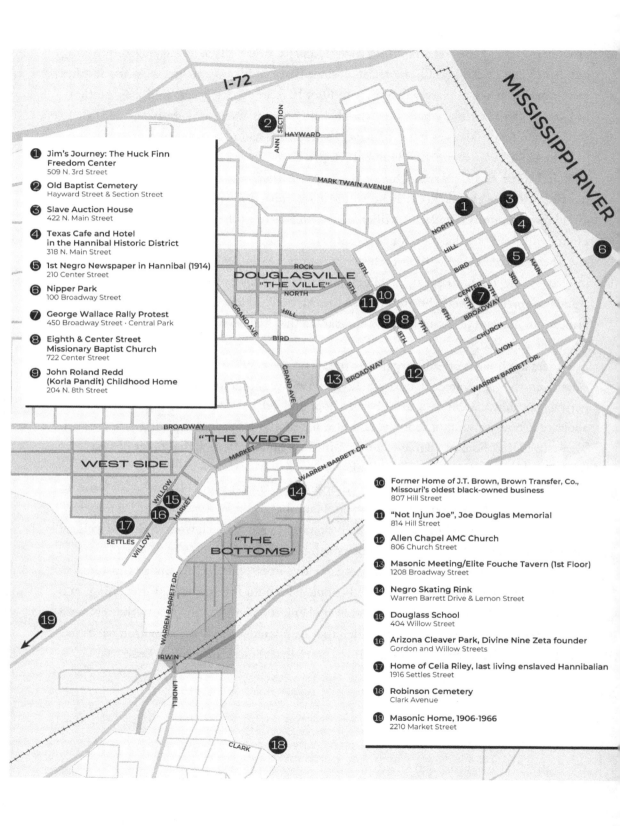

Hannibal is in northeast Missouri on the banks of the Mississippi River. Today, the estimated population is 17,300, with 15,200 white people, 1,100 Black people, and others. It should be noted that an 1860 census indicates that Blacks made up 25 percent of the population. The 1929 Colored Directory lists the population of the town as 20,000, with 4,000 Negroes.

Chapter 1

EARLY HANNIBAL

The story of early Hannibal, Missouri, cannot be told without acknowledging Hannibal's first Black citizens—the enslaved pioneers. They helped build this community, beginning with those who accompanied the town's founder, Moses Bates, when he settled the town in 1819. These enslaved people who accompanied Bates cleared the land and built the first store on Main and Hill, the main source of provisions for all early pioneers. He operated a keelboat that ran between St. Louis and Hannibal. That boat brought new settlers, as well as enslaved men, women, and children. Bates's original complement of enslaved men and women who accompanied him to Hannibal are no longer anonymous. Their names were Jemima, William, Moses, Randall, and Jacob.

In 1870, the *Hannibal Clipper* (an early newspaper in town) interviewed Jacob, who was then a free man named Jacob Lowe, who recalled being purchased by Bates at an auction in Vicksburg, Mississippi. He was just fourteen, and he left behind his parents and siblings, who mourned the departure of their son and brother. Jacob recalled working for Bates at the residence of William Clark, who was then governor of Missouri, in Jefferson City. According to the 1860 Slave Schedules, he also worked on Bates's farm with more than thirty other enslaved people. Jacob's last appearance is in the 1873 City Directory, where he is found living on North Street between North Main and Third, just a couple blocks from where Hannibal's first log cabin was built at Bird Street and Main. During the Civil War, Moses Bates fought for the Confederacy to try and retain ownership of these people. He, of course, failed. Once emancipated, Jacob lived and died in Hannibal.

Other early Black Hannibalians were brought here from Kentucky, Virginia, Tennessee, or the Carolinas, and like Jacob, they left behind friends and relatives now lost to them forever. It saddens me to think about the families that were destroyed by this forced migration.

The life of Missouri slaveholding households was different from those in the Deep South. Here, there were very few plantations, and that meant fewer slaves. Leasing enslaved people, rather than buying them, was the norm. In Hannibal's earliest days, the booming river town was ripe for this leasing system. Before the Civil War, there were five slave traders living in the town.

One 1848 ad reads: "HANDS WANTED: The subscriber wishes to employe, immediately, FIFTY Negro Men, to work on the Rail-Road. For stout, able-bodied men, higher prices will be paid than can be obtained anywhere else in this section of the country."

In 1850, there were 2,852 enslaved people in Marion County. The Polk Directory of 1859 lists thousands of enslaved people who were leased out to do the heavy lifting as the community grew. The city government, retailers, soap and tobacco manufacturers, sawmills, packing houses, railroads, builders, shippers—even individual households—all leased slaves. Surprisingly, the role of enslaved Blacks falls under the business description; they are listed as the number of "hands that were employed" to get the work done. These enslaved people built Hannibal's infrastructure, first clearing the land and building houses, then buildings, roads, and power supplies. In 1860, there were 3,017 enslaved people—1,406 males, 1,611 females. The slave population was about one-fifth of the free whites.

For example, while there is no specific number for the "hands" employed by the City Gas Light and Coke Company, it seems feasible that slave labor was utilized to complete the construction of the buildings and the laying of utility pipes throughout the town. Those same hands built many of the homes and created and laid the bricks that covered the streets. At Jim's Journey today, there's one such brick on display, pockmarked with the fingerprints of the enslaved person who made it not so long ago.

Foundries and machine shops appear to be the largest "employers" of leased slaves at this time, but these numbers still don't fully capture the community's overwhelming dependence on enslaved labor. According to the 1860 census, Hannibal had a population of nearly eight thousand white people, with forty free Blacks, including James Davis, Carter Braxton, George Bishop, Jerry Wade, John Hannox, Oliver Webb, and James Henderson, to name a few. While the census does not identify the specific number of men, women, and children in town who were enslaved at the time, it does indicate the value of enslavers' personal property and assets—meaning, the market value of the people they enslaved. Russell Moss, a farmer and pork merchant, had $50,000 worth of assets—that's a lot of people who contributed to his personal wealth. These "personal assets" fueled the community's economy.

POST-EMANCIPATION

The Civil War came to Missouri and freed more than 114,000 enslaved people on January 11, 1865. Fast forward: In 1935, at the height of the Great Depression, the Work Progress Administration (WPA), later renamed the Work Projects Administration, was created under President Franklin D. Roosevelt's New Deal. It was an agency that employed millions of job-seekers to carry out public work projects, including the construction of public buildings and roads with hundreds of local projects. Near the end of the program, the federal government decided to create jobs for writers and photographers—they were to document slavery in America. They visited every slaveholding state in an effort to interview as many formerly enslaved people as possible. Of course, by this time, most were dead, and many had been children when emancipated, so I suggest you also read those earlier versions written by the enslaved people themselves. I've heard people say that most formerly enslaved people just didn't want to talk about it—like it was their fault, and the shame of it belonged to them.

Fortunately, 2,500 former slaves agreed to talk to the WPA interviewers, and their testimonies eventually filled forty volumes. The most complete volumes are all available online. I caution you to read each one, remembering who the interviewer was and what he or she did and did not decide to document.

Employees of the Federal Writers Project arrived in Hannibal in the spring of 1936. A number of Hannibalians were interviewed: Emma Knight, William Henry Dant, Lewis Mundy, William Black, Margaret Nickens, and Clay Smith. I'd like to introduce you to three of them.

No known photograph exists of Margaret Nickens (1856–1943), but we know that she was born in Paris, Missouri, and enslaved by George Morrison and Jenna Taylor. At the time of Emancipation, Margaret was not even twelve years old. We know that free Margaret (Maggie) first married Samuel Taylor and lived in Shelbina, Missouri. They had a daughter, Lula Taylor (1869–1931). Lula was a graduate of Douglass School and ultimately became a teacher there for nearly forty years. Maggie later married Samuel Nickens (1845–1912), who lived in Hannibal, and she moved to his home on Center Street.

In this 1936 interview, she proudly announced that she had saved her money and added it to her husband Samuel Nickens's Civil War soldier pension and was able to purchase her home at 1544 or 1644 Broadway. She worked sixty years for two prominent former slaveholding families, the Dulaney and Mahan families. She last worked for George Mahan (1851–1936) until he died and she retired. She was eighty years old. She died of heart failure and is buried in the Old Baptist Cemetery right alongside her enslavers. Mrs. Nickens was a lifetime member of Allen Chapel AME Church. To this day, there stands

A WPA photograph of William Henry Dant (1835–1939). He died not long after this photograph was taken, and he was of sound mind and body, having worked hard all his life as a farmer, even as a free man. That fancy jacket is hiding his overalls.

a sign in the sanctuary of the church acknowledging her enslavement and expressing gratitude for her fifty years of service.

William Henry Dant is the great-grandfather of my husband, Joel Dant, and Joel's grandfather was William's oldest son, Charles Dant (1864–1929). One of William's great-granddaughters, Charlotte Muldrew, remembers visiting him in his little room on Hayden Street: "I know now that the container he was drinking from probably had whiskey in it—went with the pipe he was always smoking. Guess that's the secret to a long life." He died at 104 in the home of his daughter, Evalina Quesinberry.

William Henry Dant and his family were "the property" of Judge Daniel Kendrick. They were once valued at $4,300. William's parents, Joe and Susan Dant, are believed to have been brought to Missouri from Kentucky. The Dants toiled on Judge Kendrick's farm, south of Monroe City in Ralls County, until the end of the Civil War. William recounts in his WPA interview: "I was married and had three children when we was freed. The only slaves Mr. Kendrick had was my mother, brother, sister, and myself. Mr. Kendrick had three boys. Joe carried mail to Paris, and de other two, Bob and Jerome, was school teachers. We was treated fair when we behaved ourselves, but we had to be straightened out sometimes but we were not mistreated. We worked hard on the farm. I cradled wheat and plowed corn often till midnight. I also drove hogs to Palmyra and Hannibal."

Despite the long hours of hard work, Mr. Dant still found time to pick up some extra work for the enrichment of his family. As he notes, "I played fiddle for all de weddings and parties in de neighborhood. Dey paid me fifteen or twenty cents each time and I had money in my pockets all de time." This work helped support Mr. Dant, his wife, Mary Susan Thomas Dant (1846–1918), and their children after slavery ended—they were still young. He was thirty-five years old, and Mary Susan was about nineteen. As he recalls, "When we was set free dey gave us a side of meat and a bushel of meal. Dat's all we got." After Emancipation, Mr. Dant continued to work the land and ultimately purchased his own farm in Ralls County. When he grew too old for the demanding physical work the farm required, he moved to Hannibal to a family home at 2212 Spruce Street. Widowed, he then went to live with his daughter Evalina (1879–1950) and his son-in-law Edward Quisenberry (1867–1938). In the African American community in town, he found men and women who supported each other and encouraged their children to get educated. It's an interesting coincidence that Henry was born in 1835, the same year as Samuel Clemens. Accounts of his experiences during slavery are featured in the *Hannibal Courier-Post* (1937), the Missouri Historical Society, and the Library of Congress.

His son and daughter-in-law, Charles Dant and Mary (1868–1945), also farmed. They raised eleven children: Benjamin, Susan, Dora, Mabel, Ellabell, Amanda Bea, Eloise, Lydia, Ruth, Jerome, and Melvin.

Emma Knight, as an enslaved girl, was brought from Virginia to a farm near Florida, Missouri, by the Ely family. Emma, her two sisters, and her parents were the only slaves owned by Emily and Will Ely. In her WPA interview, she remembers her father being sold: "De master wanted to buy something for the farm."

Pictured here, she is a free woman living at 928 North Street with her daughter Emma Griffin and her grandson Russell Smith. Both her son and grandson likely attended the neighborhood Douglasville School at 925 Rock Street. The three of them lived here in a Douglassville home valued at one hundred dollars. They were surrounded by other formerly enslaved families: the Maxvilles, the Lasleys, the Washingtons, the Suttons, the Lears, and the Harrises. Emma is described as a widow of Abbott Knight, and she received seven dollars per month as a pension from his service in the Civil War.

In 1936, she recalled her experience with the Ely's as harsh. Her most powerful memory was of frostbitten feet: "We didn't have hardly no clothes and most of de time dey was just rags. We went barefoot even when it got real cold. Our feet would crack open from de cold and bleed. We would sit down and bawl and cry because it hurt so. Mother made moccasins for our feet from old pants." Just as powerful was the memory of arriving in Hannibal: "We come to Hannibal in an ox wagon. We put up at de barracks and den mother wen to live with Hiram Titchner. He lived right where de post office is now. I hired out to Mrs. James across de street for my clothes and schooling. Mrs. James had two girls." Mrs. Knight attended Eighth and Center Streets Church. She's buried at Old Baptist Cemetery.

For years, Hannibal's stakeholders attempted to perpetuate a myth that, with no plantations, Hannibal's "slaves" had it pretty easy. This view is insensitive to the heartache, pain, and powerlessness that were integral parts of existing as the property of someone else. The photograph of two unnamed young men—emancipated in the winter of 1865 (the Missouri Emancipation Proclamation is dated January 11, 1865) but with no boots and no overcoats—destroys that myth. In fact, I can't say with complete certainty whether these are boys or emaciated men.

While the truth of Hannibal's founding fathers as enslavers is omitted from many narratives of the town's early history, it can no longer be denied. I take every opportunity to remind individuals that if we're talking about anything built in Hannibal before 1865, it's likely that an enslaved person was involved. Yes, they were laborers, but they were also skilled tailors, seamstresses, horsemen, barbers, cooks, carpenters, brickmasons, nurses, cooks, maids, and butlers who contributed much to the community both before and immediately after Emancipation.

With the Civil War came hope. Many of our ancestors walked off the farms and away from local "employers" to join the Union soldiers who had taken over the town. When

Emma Knight (1848–1945) was about ninety years old when this photograph was taken. She appears to still be doing her own shopping, walking with the help of a cane.

Emancipation was ratified in Missouri on January 11, 1865, there were around 114,000 enslaved people in the state.

Emancipation Day! I can almost hear the cheers and shouts that would have gone up in town and across the countryside!

Yes, legalized chattel slavery ended long ago, after the Union won and after the passage of the Thirteenth, Fourteenth, and Fifteenth Amendments. However, it only ended chattel slavery—slavery in which an individual is considered the personal property of another. While painful, this lesson still needs to be taught.

HOMEOWNERSHIP AND MORE

Joe Douglas—a Black man said to be of Osage descent—drifted into Hannibal and decided to make it home. While working as a drayman (a baggage-handler) on the riverfront, Douglas was able to purchase cheap plats of land just blocks from the center of town in the incorporated hills that were not yet cleared. Making it habitable wasn't going to be easy, but it was cheap. After the Civil War, Mr. Douglas resold these plats to his newly emancipated friends and neighbors. In the process, he laid the foundations for a self-sufficient Black community with businesses, a church, a school, and neighbors reliant on each other for survival.

Yet he spent his life fighting the myth perpetuated by local stakeholders that he was the inspiration for "Injun Joe," the villain in *The Adventures of Tom Sawyer*. In fact, he arrived in Hannibal nearly a decade after Samuel Clemens left and, unlike that fictional character, Douglas never harmed anyone.

When he passed at the age of 102 in 1923, Douglas was living at 814 Hill Street. The Black doctor, Dr. McMechen, was by his bedside. According to his death certificate, Douglas died of ptomaine poisoning from eating pickled pigs' feet, a common delicacy in the early 1900s. Even in

An image of Joe Douglas (1821-1923). He is buried alongside his wife, Anna, at Mt. Olivet Cemetery. His tombstone reads, "Injun Joe." All wrong. It should read, "Joe Douglass, the real estate developer."

death, the "Injun Joe" handle stuck with him. The Black community created a memorial recognizing his contributions to the foundation of the Black community in Hannibal. It's erected near his Hill Street home in Douglasville—a neighborhood named in his honor.

Two enslaved African American boys, photographed by J. R. Shockley on Hannibal's Main Street sometime between 1860 and 1865. This photo is held in the Library of Congress.

Chapter 2

WATER, WATER EVERYWHERE

The Mississippi River is the second-longest river in North America, and it separates those of us in Hannibal from our neighbors in Illinois. It's one of the most beloved bodies of water in the country. And when I think about what I love about Hannibal, at the top of the list is the river. Waterfront renovations completed in 2020 will accommodate one of the largest cruise ships on the Mississippi River, the *Viking*, to enjoy a layover in Hannibal. A young Samuel Clemens, who grew up along its banks, once said, "the Mississippi River will always have its own way: no engineering skills can persuade it to do otherwise."

There were five slave traders living in Hannibal before the Civil War, and the Mississippi brought enslaved people north to Missouri—or it took them to even more horrific slave states downriver, dismantling entire families and causing profound pain and suffering. The Mississippi also represented hope: if a slave could make it across to the Illinois side, they'd be free, though Illinois was full of slave-catchers, and there would be a bounty on the head of anyone who escaped. Many made it, but many did not. Untold numbers of enslaved men, women, and children drowned trying to cross the mighty Mississippi to freedom. I can imagine runaways languishing or dying on Jackson Island, trying to make their way across the mile-wide river.

In 1854, a boy was born into slavery on a farm near Bush Creek in Ralls County, Missouri. His enslaved parents—Peter Paul Tolton and Martha Jane Chisley Tolton—"belonged" to the Elliotts, who were devout Catholics. The baby boy was baptized and given the name Augustus at St. Peter's Catholic Church. In the heat of the Civil War, Augustus's father ran away to join the Union Army. His father was never seen again and likely died in the war. His mother gathered her young children (Samuel, Charley,

Image of the historic Hannibal waterfront, flooded, in the 1940s.

Augustus, and Anne) and made their way about twenty miles west to the bank of the Mississippi River with an eye on freedom. It's believed that a Union soldier ferried them across. Thanks to Martha's courage, the family reached Illinois, where Augustus grew up in Quincy.

There, his Catholic faith grew stronger, but his dream of becoming a priest was unattainable in the United States. Augustus crossed the Atlantic to be ordained as a Catholic priest in Rome. It was in 1886 when he returned to the United States to serve as the country's first (publicly acknowledged) Black Roman Catholic priest. He led a congregation in Quincy for some years but was met with so much opposition that he was moved to a church in Chicago. Funny thing about Quincy: it was likely the first stop north on the Underground Railroad, and while many in the community fought for the abolition of slavery, they didn't want to learn about, live with, or praise God with Black people. Jim Crow lived very comfortably in Quincy.

Augustus was moved to St. Monica's Parish in Chicago, where "Father Gus" grew the congregation from thirty parishioners to six hundred, justifying the construction of a new church. His oratory skills are renowned. Fr. Tolton's success at ministering to Black and white Catholics quickly earned him national attention within the Catholic hierarchy. Sadly, he was only forty-three years old when he died—the cause of death was heatstroke.

Today, Fr. Tolton is on track to become the first African American saint. His canonization process is well underway in the Vatican. In 2019, he was declared venerable by Pope Francis, an important step toward his canonization.

Could be called a miracle, but Tolton isn't the only Black former slave with Hannibal ties up for sainthood in the Roman Catholic Church. Julia Greeley, born here in 1833, was taken to St. Louis and then to Denver, where she was freed and where she converted to Catholicism. She was baptized in Denver in 1880 while working for a wealthy white family. Despite her own life of poverty, she became well-known for her charitable efforts. Upon discovering Julia, the Archdiocese of Denver began the process of her canonization in 2014.

THE RELENTLESS POWER OF THE MIGHTY MISSISSIPPI

Hannibal changed with time, but the known and unknown dangers associated with the Mississippi River did not. Many tell stories of jumping from the old railroad bridge into the river for a swim. Young Ira French (known as Dale to his family), the son of Juanita and Warren French, was one victim of the river's might. In 1953, on a humid Missouri morning in July, nine-year-old Ira met his friends on the banks of the river, playing in the water and hoping to find relief from the heat. A current took him, and he never returned home. Ira's shorts washed ashore just seven miles away in Saverton a week later.

Flooding has always been a threat. To date, the worst flood in Hannibal was the flood of 1973, when the river crested at 28.59 feet. It occurred in April, and it was caused by heavy snow up north and heavy spring rain. Both Main Street and the downtown area were taken out quickly as water spilled into storefronts. No one was spared. Floodplain residents saw it coming and followed the lead of the merchants. They grabbed as many of their belongings and valuables as they could, taking them to safety upstairs if they had a second floor, or to the home of a "dry" friend or relative.

Until the relatively recent installation of levees and floodwalls, Hannibal has always been at the mercy of the Mississippi River. The annual spring flooding posed a regular challenge to many Hannibalians, especially the Black residents living in Hannibal's Fifth Ward—"the Bottoms"—a working-class community that sprung from the soggy earth of this floodplain. There was often knee-high mud for months, complicated by the fact that the streets in the Black community were unpaved. The biggest threat of flooding came from Bear Creek, a river tributary that could cause havoc. Bear Creek

Bear Creek, out of control during a recent flood that inundated the old skating rink—where Tina Turner once performed.

flows down a quarter-mile wide ravine until it reaches the rocky and dangerous banks of the Mississippi.

When the creek flooded, those who lived near it relied on neighbors and various emergency organizations for assistance. During floods, streets closed, families were stranded, and it was often the fishermen's boats that ferried stranded residents to dry ground. The Salvation Army, the Red Cross, and the Missouri National Guard all mobilized to assist the flood victims. Many had to be fed and sheltered for weeks, waiting for the water to recede so cleanup could begin.

Valarie Hawkins Shaw tells a heartwarming story of her family's spring flooding experience and their seasonal enemy, Bear Creek.

"Every time it rained, I remember Granny and my mother hopping in the car heading down to the creek to assess the water situation," Valarie recalls. "Better than any weatherman."

In her memory, the record-breaking flood of 1957 stands out. One morning in mid-March, the rain started early in the morning and didn't stop. By the evening, sheets of rain were thundering onto the family's roof and had poured several inches of water onto the streets and yards, quickly filling them with water.

Here, Bear Creek spills over onto Lindell Avenue. Rev. Minnie Smith recalls her grandmother being a victim of the 1947 flood. The house they knew and loved was turned completely around; the front door that had faced Arch Street now faced Lindell Avenue.

Bear Creek backs up quickly, and residents instinctively knew that the water was coming. They had a choice: stay or go.

"Fortunately, we lived in a two-story house. Everyone, even the kids, hurriedly gathered valuables and took them upstairs," Valarie recalls, as if it were yesterday. "I can remember carrying glass jugs of water and food upstairs to 'ride out' the flood. My grandmother was amazingly organized and ready in every way. Neighbors helping neighbors. All of us instinctively knew to open the front and back doors of our houses to let the water flow through. Experience had taught us well."

Many neighbors evacuated, but those who stayed found themselves knocking on Valarie's door, seeking refuge. Their two-story house in the Bottoms was a rarity—dry space during a spring flood.

"I can still see my Uncle Henry wading in waist-high water to get home to us," Valarie remembers. "Despite our protests, he kept coming through dangerous debris. Branches, dead fish, barrels, even furniture."

Just as they did after every flood, the residents of the Bottoms started the horrendous cleanup process. Everywhere, the water had left mud behind. It was a baptism of a different kind, a rebirth each spring.

Valarie and her big brother Patrick were kids when their mother moved them from their grandparents' house in the Bottoms. She graduated from Hannibal High School in 1969, earned a bachelor's degree from Stephens College in Columbia (where she is now on the Board of Trustees) and a master's from William Woods University. She was a trailblazing banking professional, starting out as a teller at the local Commerce Bank when it was still very rare to see a Black person sitting behind the counter of a bank. She worked in Hannibal from 1980 to 1990. Valarie retired from a thirty-six-year banking career at Commerce Bank in June 2016, having served as the executive vice president and retail director. In this capacity, she oversaw the retail sales, service, and operations for fourteen branches in the Central Missouri Region (in the Missouri counties of Boone, Moniteau, Audrain, Randolph, and Marion). Valarie was also responsible for branch security, facility management, and a couple dozen ATMs. After twenty years and numerous promotions with the Columbia branch, she became executive vice president. Though retired from the bank, she stays extremely busy in her adopted community and has assumed leadership roles in the Columbia Branch of the NAACP, the Columbia Kiwanis Club, Delta Sigma Theta Sorority, Inc. and the Links, Inc. She is also active in her church and with her family of two sons, five grandchildren, and four great-grandchildren.

Even today, Bear Creek floods almost every spring.

LET THEM EAT FISH

George Hayden was my stepfather, and my brother Ronnie's father—we all called him Dad. This photograph was taken after a day spent on the banks of the Mississippi—fishing for carp, buffalo fish, catfish, perch, and other kinds of fish I can't name. He was a good provider. He fished in the summer and hunted in the winter, and what he brought home provided many of our meals. He also worked as a laborer for the White Star Laundry. He was a World War II Army veteran. Like many folks then and now, he could best be described as one of the "working poor."

While Dad was fishing, my brothers and I busied ourselves in the park along the river—there was lots of room to run and play games. Riverfront-Nipper Park was demolished in 2017 to make way for the new marina—another local WPA Project lost forever. My brothers and I were taken to this park mainly at night while my mother was working the second shift at a local restaurant and my stepfather was desperate to get in some fishing. I have to confess that my brothers and I played in the unsupervised fountain. We loved going to the riverfront and large park; it was a beautiful, idyllic spot at the foot of Broadway on the riverfront. It included acres of grassy space, a paved walkway, the lighted water fountain, benches, and even restrooms.

Dad was only forty-three when he died of an enlarged heart. I remember the day well; it was in March, and we were in school. I ran into our neighbor and the local undertaker, Mr. Roberts, coming down our steps. He stunk of the cigar dangling from his mouth, and for no reason, he gave me a nickel. I know now that it was supposed to ease my pain of losing "Daddy." When I think about my stepfather's death, I am reminded of how our family, friends, and neighbors responded. Family came from near and far, and they stayed until after the funeral. Local friends and neighbors showed up with a dish to share, and our table and refrigerator filled up with food. Most of it was homemade: cakes, pies, and a pot of this or that. Those who couldn't cook brought bread or soda. I still try to continue that tradition. It's what we do in our time of grief. We still talk about when our much-loved "brother-cousin," Ray Robinson, passed way too soon, not even forty. We were living in Chicago then, and of course, we headed straight to his home—had to check on his mother, Chuckie, his wife, Jackie, and their children. His home quickly filled up with family and friends. In our memory, it seems like everyone showed up with one of JJ's Chicken and Fish fifty-piece pan of wings. Counting how many wings we ate that evening made us love Ray more, and we laughed until we cried.

Many Black old-timers also seem to remember a huge boulder that once stood at the riverfront at the park entrance, marking the spot where enslaved people were bought and

Left: Local sportsman, John Perkins, in 2017, with his record-breaking fifty-pound catfish. As he often puts it, "I'd be fishing now if it wasn't so cold."

Right: 1950s photograph of George Hayden (1915–1959), who was born in Youngstown, Ohio. He looks pretty proud of his morning's catch. He often got up at 5:00 a.m. to get his favorite spot on the river.

Me and my brothers, Ronnie, Larry, and Mike, taken at Nipper Park. In the background is the beautiful, very photogenic—and unsupervised—park fountain.

Rosa Ford Taylor (1924–2018) on a visit to the park, a lovely spot to take visitors with its paved walkway and benches.

Rosa Ford's unidentified friend, also enjoying the park.

The exact location, church, and the individuals in this photograph, which was taken somewhere along Bear Creek in the late 1800s, are unidentified. River baptisms were common for generations until church finances enabled them to build an indoor baptismal. Ruth Thompson Baker (1919–2017) would beam when she recalled that, as a girl, she was baptized in Bear Creek.

sold. In 1934, the Missouri Historical Society replaced the boulder with a cast-iron historical marker. It read:

> The Mark Twain cave is located two and one half miles south from this spot. From a little log house across the river three miles north from this place, Mark Twain started Huckleberry Finn on his trip to freedom. Tom Sawyer's Island is southeast from here one mile down the river. Here Huckleberry Finn and Niggar Jim stopped for a few days on their way down the Mississippi.

This racist sign greeted visitors from all over the country, and for more than fifty years, it was the only official reference to African Americans in Hannibal. It's not a surprise, since the Mahans, a former slaveholding family and pillars of the community, were responsible for the plaque. At the time, George Mahan was president of the Missouri Historical Society.

WILLIAMSVILLE

Williamsville was home to another pocket of Black residents. The neighborhood clings to the banks of Minnow Creek, but the creek seldom causes any major flooding issues here. Their homes were on Carroll, Hawkins, Garth, and Woodson streets. "Funny how we never left the neighborhood, plenty of playmates in its four blocks. I didn't know any of the Westside kids until we started school together," lifelong resident Valarie Mosley says, reflecting on seventy years of memories in the area. She is the fourth generation to live in the home built by her grandparents, Nathan Holman and Clarabelle Williams. She fondly reflects on her neighbors through the years—the ones on both sides of the creek: the Stallings, who had eleven children; three Williams families; the Hawkins; the Elys; the Wards; the Abbeys; and a couple white families.

I enjoyed listening as she shared her experience of playing in the creek and on the bridge. What she told me contained more than the story of one woman's life. It is a portrait of the life and culture on the creek. Her reminiscences include important details about daily life: "We set up minnow traps and waded in the water, homes lacked air conditioning and it was the only place to cool off on hot summer days." On Sunday mornings, the sound of gospel music filled the whole neighborhood—coming from every home. "Mahalia Jackson, Shirley Caesar, Andraé Crouch were my favorites," Valarie says. By about 10:00 a.m., it got quiet when everyone was getting ready for church. "There is a church in the neighborhood we all attended—Allen Chapel AME Church built here in 1966. It used to be downtown where the new post office is."

Valarie once asked me to take a photograph of Missouri's oldest pedestrian swinging bridge on Carroll Street. She was very anxious, knowing the city had its eyes on it as another demolition project. Having played in the creek and on the bridge without incident for so many years, she didn't see its deterioration as a threat. She thought more about saving this historical treasure.

One day in 2018, Valarie looked up and the Carroll Street Bridge was gone. She and her neighbors had no say in the decision. It was no longer available to the residents on either side of the creek. This walkway over the creek was gone forever.

An image of the suspension/swinging pedestrian bridge at the foot of Carroll Street over Bear Creek. Decades ago, the big swinging bridge was one of a dozen wire suspension bridges in Missouri, most of which were built by the same man, Joseph A. Dice. Dice constructed more than forty wire suspension bridges in mid-Missouri between 1895 and 1940. Suspension bridges, which are also known as swinging bridges because there is no support underneath them, really do swing. Dice hung his bridges on massive steel wire cables running between two towers. The cables create a catenary chain—the curve produced when a flexible wire hangs from two fixed supports. Vertical suspension cables connect the bridge's deck to the catenary chain. These cables get shorter toward the bridge's middle, creating the deck's arch. Besides adding to the excitement (or terror) of crossing the bridge, this arch allows the deck to flatten a little with heavy loads, enhancing the bridge's strength.

Chapter 3

A COMMUNITY WITHIN

Even though enslaved people had built Hannibal from the ground up, as a community, they were kept from reaping the benefits of their labor. So their descendants built a second Hannibal, and with it, they provided us with a future. In conversations about race and racism in America, a term we all know is "Jim Crow." It refers to legalized segregation from about 1877 to 1965. It included a variety of discriminatory laws, rules, regulations, and customs meant to keep Black folks in their place. No race mixing. But Jim Crow was more than a series of rigid anti-Black laws. It was a way of life. Under Jim Crow, African Americans were relegated to the status of second-class citizens. These laws and rules of etiquette were driven by fear of the marginalization of the white race—does that sound familiar?

When most people think of Jim Crow, they only think of the anti-Black laws relating to public transportation, jobs, housing, the military, and schools. Most folks don't realize that these rules separated people into races in all of daily life—parks, libraries, prisons, hospitals, and juries. These laws were on the books in southern states and understood throughout the rest of the country. In Hannibal, more often than not, there were unwritten rules about what you could and couldn't do. Jim Crow etiquette—where to walk, how to address white people—lingered on for generations. In Jim's Journey, I have a sign which reads, "Even when you went to work you had to come in the back door."

The dangers associated with this period were also very real. In fact, violence or the threat of violence was the key to making Jim Crow so effective for so long. More than thirty-three thousand Black men, women, and children were tortured, burned, or lynched across the United States during this period, which also gave rise to the KKK and other hate groups. Never forget that Emmett Till's alleged crime—for which he was murdered—was simply speaking to a white woman. Many Blacks migrated to northern cities, forced to leave family and the homes they had lived in for generations.

In Hannibal, Blacks quickly learned that white people weren't going to birth or bury us, teach us to read or write, police us or put out our fires, deliver our mail or milk, allow us to purchase groceries or eat in one of their restaurants with dignity, or teach us about the love and glory of God. In response, we developed a community within, and in comes the Colored Directory and the *Green Book*. Jim Crow laws had moved us into self-contained neighborhoods, where we found places to retreat to with dignity and without fear.

Segregation was meant to box us in and keep us out of the mainstream. And in many ways, it did. But it also gave birth to an enterprising generation of young African American men and women in the earliest decades of the twentieth century. They not only provided life's necessities but also built our Black institutions. They gave us hope and a sense of pride. Delegated to the fringes of the broader community, church leaders, business leaders, and others stepped up.

According to the 1927 Colored Directory, among the four thousand Black citizens of Marion County, 65 percent were homeowners. Imagine that: one generation after slavery and able to purchase a home, albeit only in one of our segregated neighborhoods. Barriers had been erected, forcing the Black community to make its own way. And we did. In some instances, we grew our own; most of our teachers, for example, were the first post-Emancipation generation and Douglass School graduates who had gone away to college and returned armed with teaching credentials. We recruited school administrators, doctors, nurses, dentists, undertakers, mailmen, night watchmen (police), and firemen. Entrepreneurs sprouted up in our business district and neighborhoods all over town, with schools, churches, cemeteries, taxis, grocery stores, bars, restaurants, beauty shops, and barbershops.

The 1927 Colored Directory, published by a local African American printer, Wright's Publishing. It lists the names and addresses of local Black residents of Hannibal and Marion County (Monroe City, Palmyra, New London, Shelbina). It also lists advertisers of businesses who will "happily serve Coloreds" as well as ads for many Black-owned businesses. And lastly, there is a biographic sketch of Hannibal's most prominent Black residents.

Reo Cabs - Phone 18

COLORED DIRECTORY

Also Information and Facts of Interest to 4,000 Colored People of

HANNIBAL, MISSOURI

AND MARION COUNTY

Together with Buyer's Guide of Best Business Places in the City.

ISSUED JULY 1927

OUR SIMPLE CREED

To strive constantly to establish ourselves high in the esteem of those requiring our services.

To perform our tasks in such a way as to lighten the burden of sorrow that the bereaved must bear.

Prompt and Efficient Service

FREE CHAPEL

EARL HARRIS

UNDERTAKER

AMBULANCE SERVICE

Office Phone 188   Res. 1393J

302 S. Fifth St., Hannibal, Mo.

Most of these "Colored places" have since been demolished or significantly changed, but it is important to emphasize: Black residents built a thriving community of citizens within the constraints of racial segregation!

NEWSPAPERS: THE FIRST OPPORTUNITY TO TELL OUR OWN STORY

African American newspapers began before the Civil War—their focus, of course, was freedom. In 1827, free Blacks Samuel Cornish and John B. Russwarm started the first African American periodical, called *Freedom's Journal*. It led the fight for liberation and human rights, published articles that demonstrated racial pride, and informed readers of events affecting the African American community. The *North Star*, founded by Frederick Douglass, was another of our earliest newspapers, but the lack of a reading customer base meant short-lived success for many of these publications. By the Civil War, forty Black newspapers were being published, but it wasn't until the 1920s and 1930s that the Black press earnestly began. The consumer base increased as Black people became readers and migrated from fields to more urban areas. It was at a time when white papers either ignored Black America or perpetuated myths and stereotypes. It was critical that we tell our own story, promote our own, uplift our community and report on topics and people important to its readership.

Imagine my surprise when I learned of the *Home Protective Record*, a weekly Black newspaper published in Hannibal in the early 1900s. It was financed by the Negro Newspaper Association. Rev. Cyrus R. McDowell (1852–1950), pastor of the Eighth and Center Streets Missionary Baptist Church, was the newspaper's publisher. Unfortunately, not even a year after the paper initially appeared, there was a fire in the office. Rev. McDowell's

Employees captured in the composing room of Hannibal's first Negro newspaper, the *Home Protective Record*. The office was located at 200 Center Street in 1914. Pictured here are Rev. McDowell's twenty-seven-year-old son, a Douglass School graduate, Edward McDowell, and the newspaper staff.

son, Edward McDowell (1886–1914), died of the burns he received from the explosion of wood alcohol used in the printing plant. Hannibal's first Negro newspaper ceased publication. McDowell had accomplished much at Eighth and Center, and in 1916, he moved to Helping Hand Baptist. He built the Lyon Street church and parsonage. He also enjoyed leadership roles in numerous fraternal organizations. McDowell came to Hannibal from Kentucky and lived here twenty-six years.

There was a second Black newspaper, the *Hannibal Register*, published by George Hannibal Wright (1888–1962), his wife Rose (1896–1979), and their children. It was the longest-running Black newspaper in town. George was the son of the formerly enslaved Sam Wright (1842–1918) and Julia Wright (1848–1919).

George and Rose had married in Ann Arbor, Michigan, and moved to Hannibal in 1918. They began their life here in Douglasville (690 North Street) and lived there for nineteen years before moving to 2204 Spruce Street. George and his eleven children were all Douglass School graduates.

Besides editing and publishing a weekly newspaper, Mr. Wright directed the publication of the town's Colored Directory and several Douglass School yearbooks. His publishing business was at 1228 Broadway, and the newspaper was a lifetime member of the Association of Negro Newspapers. The publishing business ran until 1941, when they moved to Michigan (where George and Rose had met and married years before), leaving an impressive legacy in Hannibal. The family publishing business continues to this day.

George Hannibal Wright. He and his wife, Rose Trott Wright, had eleven children: Charles, George, DuBois, Samuel, John, Booker, Francis, Harriet, Isabelle, Maria, and Anna.

THE WEDGE: 1200-1218 BROADWAY

For a number of years, the hub of Hannibal's Black economy was called the Wedge, named for the wedge-shaped corner where North Broadway converged with Market Street.

James Thomas Brown (1874–1948) is credited as the architect of the early brick structures that were built here around 1905. The original buildings were just a half-block long. On the ground floor, businesses thrived, operated by local Black entrepreneurs and professionals. The second floors were apartment homes to many working-class families as well as clubs and fraternal groups. While it's impossible to learn the specifics, it's obvious that the Prince Hall Masons were involved in the construction—see the Blazing Star symbol on the front of the largest building, representing their presence.

This history of the Wedge goes back to Hannibal's earliest days, as the business district expanded west from the river. While we owned this section of Broadway, there were even some Black businesses on the Market Street side and scattered around town, wherever there was a pocket of Black residents.

After much controversy, this historic landmark was demolished in 1982. "Urban renewal," they called it. The half-block area on the north side of Broadway was razed for the National Grocery Store; they were desperate to move from their flood-prone

The businesses at 1200-1218 Broadway, including a grocery store, a funeral parlor, a beauty shop, a barbershop, and restaurants and taverns, all operated by African Americans.

Arthur "Ted" Green (1909-1969) was a highly successful civic leader and businessman. He owned several businesses through the years, and his chief cook and bottle washer was his aunt, Susie Green (1887-1954). In the 1920s, Ted Green owned the Spotless Kitchen at 112 Hill Street (Hannibal's Historic District), and years later, at the time of his death, he owned Green's Cleaners on Lindell Avenue. He was married to Katherine King Green. The couple made their home on E. Gordon Street and were faithful members of Eighth and Center Streets Missionary Baptist Church. They had three children: Shelia, Janet, and John Jr. A true entrepreneur and church and community leader, Ted served two terms as president of the local NAACP.

Wilbert Gipson, a chauffeur, in 1954. He's posing in front of Elite Tavern, photographed here coming from Charles McElroy's funeral—the Elite sign can be seen in the window over his right shoulder. See the alley next to the tavern—a lot of gambling, with dice as the game of choice, and even a few altercations went on here.

Lyon Street location and colluded with the city to make it happen. There was much public controversy when the city designated the area "blighted." The city also designated Maple Avenue and Girard Street as blighted and destroyed more homes, as well as the Grants Tourist Home and the local Colored American Legion.

The Wedge may be gone, but its spirit is not. That spirit was never confined to one specific place anyway. Since the earliest days of Hannibal—the Bottoms, Douglasville, the Westside, and more—Black Hannibalians have always found a way out of no way.

Fouche's Elite Tavern at 1208 Broadway was where you could get a sandwich, a nickel bag of chips, and a cold drink (Pepsi, whiskey, or bottled or draft beer). You could also play a game of pool or even get a shoeshine. It was owned by Choteau Fouche (1891–1976) and his wife, Grace (1909–2003). Like all local bars, the walls of their establishment were covered with liquor ads, and the place smelled of beer, whiskey, and cigarettes. It had worn wooden floors and a beautifully polished bar running almost the entire length of the building, and there were plenty of stools and extra tables for patrons who wanted a little privacy. There was an awesome jukebox—a guy came in once a month to change out the newest R&B hits—but the real attraction was its vintage pool table that had a huge Stag Beer chandelier hanging above it. It cost a quarter per game and attracted players both young and old. The chandelier now hangs in Jim's Journey.

Buddies getting together for a drink at Fouche's Elite Tavern. This photograph includes (left to right) an unknown individual, Walter Sutton, owner Choteau Fouche, and his brother Robert Fouche.

Grace Fouche, posing with Clydesdales in front of the family business, Fouche's Elite Tavern at the Wedge, during the July Fourth parade in 1950.

Choteau Fouche, with first wife, Bessie Fouche, also owned the Choteau, an earlier tavern/restaurant at 110 Bird Street. This savvy businessman opened his establishment near LuLubelles, a brothel. Both catered to the railroad employees. The Fouches were business owners and civic leaders for more than sixty years. Chote was born in Hannibal to John and Laura Fouche, one of five children. Charles, William, and Chote all attended Douglass School. Chote's oldest brother, John Gordon Fouche, married Mollie Vaughn in Hannibal—soon after the marriage, they moved to Chicago. Chote remained in Hannibal for a number of years, before he joined his brother in Chicago, where he married and divorced. He also met his future wife, Grace Range, there. Grace was from Kansas City. She was seventeen years younger than Chote and a 1928 Lincoln High School graduate. They married in 1942 and were back in Hannibal running the business at the Wedge by 1950. Together, they raised one adopted daughter, Bonnie Green Dean (1930–2015).

John Woods (1911–1960), "Shorty." Shorty was a favorite home barber if you wanted a bowl or a bald haircut—very little skill required. It was done by putting a cooking pot of a fit size to the level of the ears, and all the hair below the rim was cut or shaved off.

Family owned and operated, "the Cafe" was a place where families came for a meal and where teenagers regularly hung out. Here, you see Louis (1900–1983) and his wife, Margaret Williams Dixon (1909–1986), proudly photographed in front of the establishment they owned for a number of years. I believe this photograph was taken in the sixties. Going here meant we didn't have to go to the white restaurants (for a carryout), where we weren't welcome, or to

the skating rink, where we either had to go on "Negro Skate Nite" or where we had to bring our own skates. This Dixon family was from Palmyra, Missouri, nine miles from Hannibal. They had seven children—Louis, Joseph, Edna, Alice, Nancy, Louis, and Dixie, all of whom worked here and helped sustain the business.

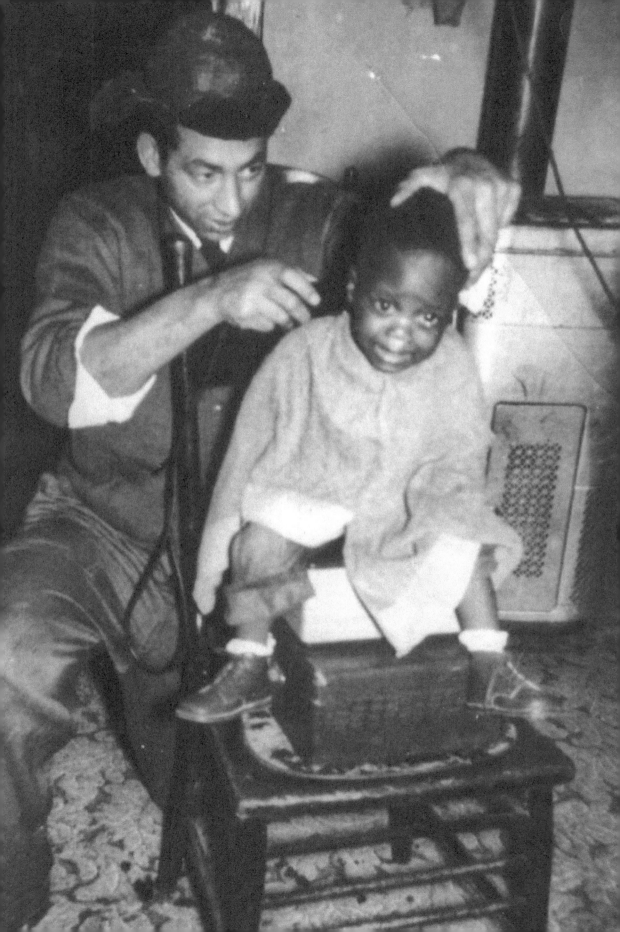

Right: Elizabeth Bell (1892–1978) had a beauty shop at the Wedge, and she proudly advertised her credentials from the Poro Beauty School in St. Louis. Poro was founded by Annie Malone, one of the earliest Black millionaires in the country. How ironic that her wealth came from the effort to make Negro hair straight and thus make us more acceptable to white people.

Left: An unidentified, unhappy customer getting his hair cut by Albert Long (1916–2003), one of several barbers employed by Mr. J. P. Morgan Barbershop at 1214 Broadway.

Here are a few more Black-owned local businesses, some at the Wedge, compiled from various sources throughout the years:

THE WEDGE, 1200–1230 BROADWAY

1208 Broadway: Fouche's Elite Tavern and Pool Hall, Little Egypt Bar
1208 Broadway (upstairs): Negro Masonic Lodge
1210 Broadway, Rose Garden: Hobbs Grocery, Lewis Smokehouse, Bummer Lasley's Tavern, Clay's Barbershop
1212 Broadway: Matties Paradise, Blakey's Barbershop
1214 Broadway: Clay's Barbershop, Lottie's Beauty Shop, Bell's Beauty Parlor, Morgan Barbershop
1214 Broadway (upstairs): United Brothers Fellowship Hall UBF
1216 Broadway: People's Grocery, Ted's Olympic Tavern, De-Luxe Lunch, Herb Hopkin's Tavern, the Coffee Cup, Dixon's Cafe, Sugar Shack
1218 Broadway: George Roberts Funeral Home, Robinson Mortuary
1228 Broadway: Wright's Publishing
1230 Broadway: Office of Dr. H. B. McMechen
1230 Broadway (upstairs): Odd Fellows Hall, Cavalier's Club, Vergie and Vernie Hale's Taxi
1234 Broadway: Fred McKinney Attorney, Taylor Cafe

BLACK-OWNED BUSINESSES IN OTHER PARTS OF HANNIBAL

302 S. Fifth Street: Earl Harris, Undertaker
410 N. Ninth Street: P. F. Dealy Grocery
413 N. Ninth Street: Isaac Haley Trucking
900 N. Ninth Street: Crystal Ice Company
600 Fifteenth Street: McElroy Hot Tamales Vendor
216 S. Arch Street: M. A. Lewis, Douglass School Principal
112 Bird Street: Green's Spotless Kitchen
306 Broadway: Joseph Pelham, Notary Public
514 Broadway: Washington Donley Restaurant, Black's Barbershop
2720 Carrol Street: Ruben Stallings Trucking
210 Center Street: *Home Protective* newspaper
1216 Center Street: Dr. Fox, surgeon and pharmacist
1618 Center Street: Robinson Mortuary
1217 Church Street: Dr. H. B. McMechen
Church and Eleventh: Austin Grocery Store
1218 Girard: American Legion Post #55
1328 E. Gordon Street: Willie Reed Pool Hall
2006 Gordon Street: Poro Beauty Parlor
1 Hoggs Row: Howard's Cafe
9 Hoggs Row: Blakey's Grocery
110 Hill Street: Amber Transfer
115 Hill Street: Shamrock Rooming House
115 Hill Street: Blue Haven Rooms
118 Hill Street: Perry Ambers Transfer
807 Hill Street: Brown and Sons Transfer
2103 Irvin Street: Harris Grocery
408 Lemon Street: Walter White Cafe
600 Lemon Street: Huff's Grocery, Jiffy Cleaners
180 Green Street: Elite Grocery
1216 North Street: Earl Harris Undertaker, Hannibal Directory-Eugene Lucas Publisher, Harris Rooms
318 N. Main: Texas Cafe, Fred Long Restaurant
318a N. Main: Long's Hotel
405 N. Main: Palace Barbershop, King's Barbershop & Pool Hall
1402 Paris Avenue: Redmond Theater
1516 Pleasant: Henderson Transfer
1108 Rock Street: David Anderson & Sons Trucking
205 S. Main: J. Cartwright Restaurant
206 S. Main: John Price Billiards
317 S. Main: Southside Shoeshine Parlor
1920 Texas: Williams Transfer
111 Wardlaw: Grants Colored Nursing Home
618 Wardlaw: Miss Cleotha Transfer
Outskirts of Hannibal: UBF Home, Masonic Home

DELIVER OUR BABIES AND KEEP US ALIVE

It isn't news that many herbals, plant, and non-plant remedies were used by African Americans during slavery. Methods like these demonstrate how the enslaved were responsible for their own medical care and some remedies that continue today. They have even had a resurgence. My mom, in all her wisdom, once said to me, "Faye, they call it PRACTICING medicine," in response to a complaint about doctors' lack of knowledge. Mom's scrapbook contained an article about Cecilia Riley, Hannibal's oldest "slave." She claims to have delivered one thousand babies over the course of her 116 years.

As some health care systems today seem to be committed to addressing health care disparities, it should be noted that racism and disparities are not new, and neither is distrust in the medical system. Many Hannibalians grew up with separate hospitals for Black people, or segregated wings, waiting areas, and patient rooms—even separate china. Those days, triage was based on color rather than level of need.

Most African Americans can share horror stories of discriminatory health care and segregated hospital wards, where Colored adults and children were often relegated to beds in cold and drafty spaces away from white patients, often filthy and understaffed. As a six-year-old with pneumonia, I can clearly remember being in an overcrowded room with a boy my age and two very old men, whose hacking and coughing kept me up all night. Despite the coloring books and Jell-O, I couldn't wait to get out of there.

Local doctors, nurses, and even undertakers were either born and raised here, or were recruited and became Hannibal's leading citizens. Our Black doctors were well respected, living in the nicest houses and driving late-model cars.

Most doctors treated patients in their homes or offices but were not hesitant about making house calls. Many of their patients were formerly enslaved Hannibalians. Most remained here for many years, became civic leaders, sent their children to the segregated Douglass School, and retired and died here. Their caregiving was hampered by their lack of hospital privileges—segregated health care wouldn't have it any other way.

Dr. Osceola Queen (1865–1927) was Hannibal's first Black doctor. Recruited from Texas, he and his wife, Leah (1879–1948), arrived in Hannibal about 1893, soon after his 1891 Meharry Medical College graduation. Meharry Medical College is a private, historically-Black medical school affiliated with the United Methodist Church and located in Nashville, Tennessee. It was founded in 1876 and was the first medical school for African Americans in the South.

Dr. Queen and Leah had two children, Velma and Manzilla, and Dr. Queen worked from a two-story brick home at 1235 Lyon Street. Both of the children graduated from Douglass School. Velma graduated from Howard University and returned to Hannibal

Parent-Teacher Association

Seated, left to right: Mrs. J. Crowe, Mrs. N. J. Bullock, Mrs. J. N. Davis, Dr. A. W. Fox, Mrs. M. Griggsby, Mrs. M. Alexander, and Mrs. P Demic

Standing, left to right: Rev. M. M. Matthews, Mrs. V. Hale, Mrs. M. M Matthews, Mrs. F. Allen, Mrs. C. B. Walker, Mrs. E. Allen, and Mr. C. B. Walker, Principal.

as a Douglass School first-grade teacher for more than thirty years. Manzilla, like his father, is also a graduate of Meharry—the dental college—and he returned to Hannibal briefly to become our first Black dentist before eventually settling in Kansas City. It is said Dr. Queen died in the parking lot of Levering Hospital—in 1927 he wasn't allowed in to be treated there. Dr. Queen and his wife, Leah, have the most prominent headstone in Robinson Cemetery.

Then there was Dr. Alonzo Fox, a pharmacist, surgeon, and anesthetist. Born in 1892 in Hannibal, he and his twin brother, Alfonso, were both 1909 graduates of Douglass School. Alfonso became a minister, and Alonzo decided to study medicine. Like most Black doctors in the early nineteenth century, Alonzo graduated from Meharry Medical College in Nashville. In Hannibal, he and his wife, Jessie, first worked out of their home at 1216 Center Street until a local undertaker, Mr. Sephus, purchased the building at 1731 Market Street, where he opened an office.

Dr. Fox and Jessie had three children who, like their father, graduated from Douglass. The family was also very active in the community and their church, Allen Chapel AME Church. They were very active in the NAACP, the PTA, and fraternal organizations. After retirement, he moved to Chicago to be near his children and brother, Rev. Alfonso, who died in 1962. Dr. Alonzo died in 1972.

Black nurses were not welcome in Hannibal hospitals, despite their solid education and training at one of the country's best and busiest hospitals. Fannie Perkins Griffin was a 1952 graduate of Homer G. Phillips in St. Louis, the first teaching hospital west of the Mississippi that recruited, hired, and trained thousands of Black doctors, nurses, and technicians from all over the country. It was the only public hospital for African Americans until 1979, when the city still had segregated facilities. Fannie worked at St. Elizabeth's Hospital but spent most of her career at

Seated, left to right: Mrs. Hiawatha Crow, Mrs. Emily Bullock, Mrs. Winifred Davis, Dr. A. W. Fox, Mrs. Major Griggsby, Mrs. Addie Alexander, Mrs. Peter Demic. Standing, left to right: Rev. Michael Matthews, Mrs. Bessie Hale, Mrs. Matthews, Mrs. Evalina Allen, Mrs. C. B. Walker, Mrs. E. Allen and Mr. C. B. Walker, principal.

the Hannibal Diagnostic Center, where she retired. She married Bobby Griffin, and they had two daughters, Angela and Terri.

Dr. William C. Conway graduated from the Meharry Medical College School of Dentistry in 1922 and practiced in Hannibal for more than thirty years. His first office was at the Wedge, but he later moved to an office on Market Street. A notice in his office famously read:

NOTICE

I do not fill teeth.

No work on children.

No night work.

No Sundays.

No Thursdays.

I do not like to repair plates I did not make in the first place.

Repairs are nothing but a headache for dentists.

Dr. William C. Conway (1889-1966), a World War I veteran, community leader, Mason, and our dentist for many years. Photographed here with other local Masons.

BURY US

Hannibalian Joshua Burton (1843–1932) was born a slave and brought to Hannibal from Kentucky. We know that he is identified in the 1859 City Directory as an undertaker, but we have no record of where or how he was trained. He married Winnie, with whom he had two children, Maggie and Samuel. The family lived on what was then Washington Street, and most of his neighbors were also formerly enslaved. Living with him in 1900 were his wife and son Samuel, along with Samuel's wife and five children. I wonder how many enslaved men, women, and children he buried—there are many death certificates of people buried in Old Baptist Cemetery that list him as the undertaker. Joshua died a resident of the Masonic Home on the outskirts of town.

Another of our earliest undertakers was Earl Harris (1893–1963), who was born in Hannibal and lived with his formerly enslaved parents in Douglasville. He was one of eight children. We know he attended Douglass, and while we still don't know much about

Dr. Harvey Blaine McMechen (1885–1951), impeccable in dress and manner. He graduated from Meharry Medical College in 1911 and trained in a segregated hospital in Kansas City. He built the home that he and his wife, Hullsee (1887–1952), lived in at 1217 Church Street with their daughter, Mary June McMechen (1921–2006). He treated Hannibal families for thirty-nine years and was a very active leader in the national Prince Hall Mason fraternal organization, as well as civic, religious, and professional organizations. Mary June excelled as an accomplished soprano, performing all over the United States and Europe. Another daughter, Juliette, died in infancy and is buried at Old Baptist. Dr. McMechen's office was at 1230 Broadway.

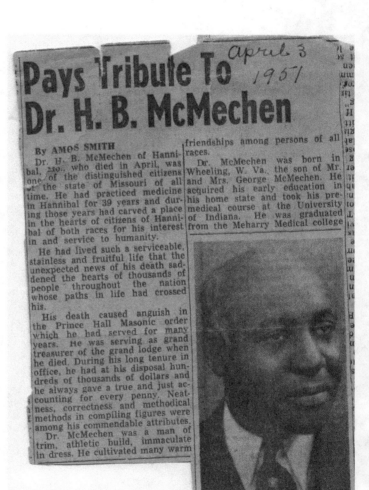

his training, we know that he is identified as an undertaker with the O'Donnell Funeral Home in the 1920s; his role was to service the Colored community. He and his wife, Elsie (1908–1964), had one son, Carl. In 1940, Earl's occupation is listed as policeman, and he is later listed as a truck driver for the City Street Department. He's described on his 1917 draft card as a single, tall, "Ethiopian" working at the Ilasco Cement Plant. I'm going to take from this that Earl was a reliable hardworking man who didn't want to be an undertaker forever.

Another Douglasville resident, George E. Roberts, lived at 1104 North Street and was a fixture in Hannibal for many years. It seems he arrived here with his entire family from Clarksville, Missouri, including his formerly enslaved parents and his two brothers. His brother William Roberts was listed as a mailman when he died in 1923. George has the distinction of owning the longest-running funeral parlor in Missouri. The Robert's Funeral Parlor at 1218 Broadway operated from 1910 to 1965. In his fifty years as an undertaker, Mr. Roberts buried many formerly enslaved men, women, and children, and their final resting place is the now defunct Old Baptist Cemetery, as well as Robinson Cemetery. Mr. Roberts and his wife, Bertha Brooks (1884–1978), had two children, Mary Roberts Williams and George Brooks Roberts, both Douglass School graduates. He was a well-respected civic leader. In 1954, he was appointed by Governor Phil Donnelly to the Board of Curators at Lincoln University.

Mr. Roberts, who was known to me as "the rich neighbor," was a Douglasville neighbor, and we could see his house from our porch. In the summer, if we determined no one was home, we would climb his fence and pilfer cherries and apples from his trees. It shames me to say that this was usually on Sunday mornings, as he and his wife were faithful members of Eighth and Center Streets Missionary Baptist Church—we weren't.

Dr. Cornelius Welch (1911-1993) at the home of a patient in 1957. He and his wife, Florence, lived in the community at 2101 Spruce Street. He treated his patients at his house or visited them in their homes. Photo courtesy of the Missouri Photo Workshop.

Left: Fannie Griffin studied nursing at the Homer G. Phillips Hospital in St. Louis. She and other local Negro nurses were forced to start their nursing careers on the other side of the river, and in her case, her first job was in Quincy, Illinois.

I recall my first meeting with him in 1959 after my stepfather died of a heart attack. It was heartbreaking, and it was Mr. Roberts who I encountered as I strolled up the sidewalk coming home from school. I found him on our porch, where he broke the news about my stepfather. This was not the only tragic death in our neighborhood that year; our neighbors Van and Ruth Smith lost their twelve-year-old daughter, Norma, to pneumonia.

After Mr. Roberts retired in 1965, another undertaker, Edward Robinson (1916–1984), purchased the mortuary at 1218 Broadway. He was there until the Wedge was demolished in 1982. He then moved the business to 1116 Center Street. It appears to be a home in a residential zone, and for that reason, the courts wouldn't allow the home to be used for a business. Mr. Robinson died less than six months later.

William R. Sephus, formerly of Canton, Missouri, was a 1927 graduate of Douglass School who graduated from the School of Mortuary Science in St. Louis. He lived in Hannibal with his wife, Rosalie Jones, a native Hannibalian.

Right: Dr. Cornelius Welch (1926–1980) pays Bessie Hale (1896–1984) a house visit in 1957. Photo courtesy of the Missouri Photo Workshop.

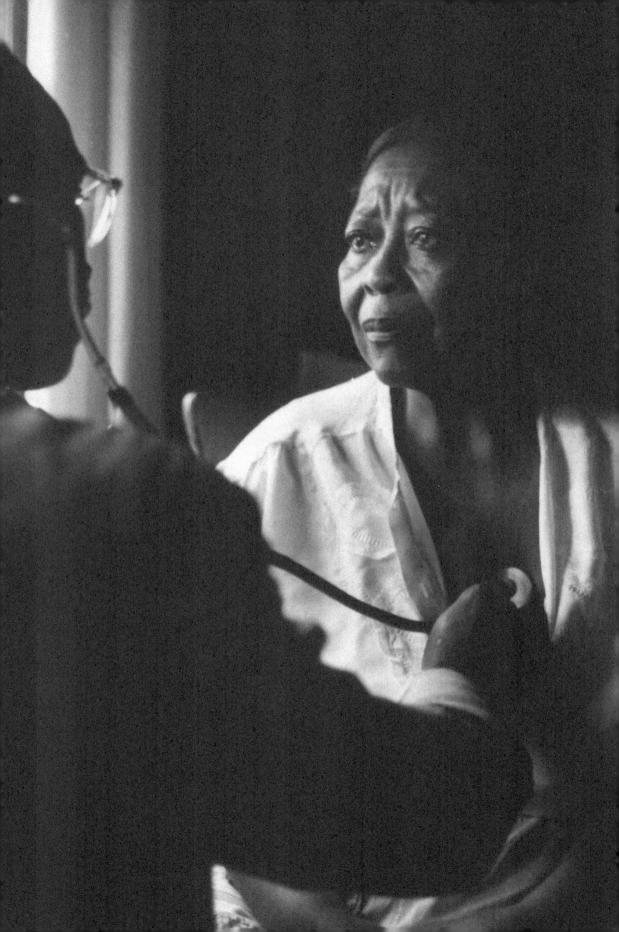

They had two daughters, Marie and Marjorie. He opened the first Sephus Funeral Home at 810 North Street. In the 1940s, he purchased the property at 1631 Market Street. Sephus remodeled the Market Street property, made Gilbert Tate a partner, and the new business became Sephus and Tate Mortuary. In the early fifties, Sephus opened another mortuary in Mexico, Missouri. In addition to his business ventures, he was also involved in the community as president of the Douglass School PTA; an officer for the community chest; an elder, choir director, board president at the Second Christian Church; and a president of the local NAACP.

The Old Baptist Cemetery was the original resting place of many Black Hannibalians—most of whom were formerly enslaved—who were laid to rest there alongside their enslavers. In 1921, Lee and Laura Robinson purchased three acres of land to be used to bury our own with care and dignity. The existing local cemeteries may have had a Colored section, located as far as possible from the white section. This property is located in Oakwood at the top of Clark Street. It's been more than ten years since it accepted burials, but it remains a significant African American historical site. Descendants from near and far still visit, perform maintenance, and decorate graves. The veterans get a flag, and the others get flowers.

Plot owners listed on the original cemetery plat include some familiar names: George Bell, William Webster, Nelson Query, Mrs. Lottie Johnson, Misses Elizabeth and Rosalie Jones, Jesse Letcher, W. R. Harrington, John Hueston, Mrs. Warren Clay, Nathan Holman, Mabel Sanders, Charles Settles, James Johnson, John Miles, Robert Taylor, Dr. O. C. Queen, James Starks, Sylvester Robinson, A. L. Robinson, Emma Jackson, Mrs. Maggie Nickens, Howard Williams, Artemas McFadden, James Henderson, Nelson Crow, Laura Hughes, Tom Allen, Andrew Tyler, Benjamin Morrison, Mrs. Henry McElroy, Sonnie Britts, Mrs. Lizzie Newberry, and Arthur Morrison.

POLICE OUR OWN ONLY

Esque Douglas (1876–1944) was the first Black sheriff in Marion County. Douglas was one of many African American night watchmen (policemen), along with Sam Hobbs, Earl Harris, and Charlie McElroy, all hired to police only the Black community. Not surprisingly, early Black law enforcement officers were not allowed to carry a gun or arrest or otherwise police white residents.

Officer Cass Jones was not the first Black police officer in Hannibal, but he was the first with all duties and responsibilities of the other officers.

THE HELP

For many years, most Blacks in Hannibal were employed by the town's white families as domestics, laundresses, yardmen, janitors, chauffeurs—their job was to make life easier for whites who could afford it. Every once in a while, I will meet someone who shares with me a "beautiful" story of the Black person who was employed by their mother. Some are oblivious to the pain their words cause, though others seem to get it. A coworker at the high school told me with a sense of pride how much she loved Winnie (Miss Winnie to us Colored kids) and how happy she was when "Mother let Winnie go with us to the Community Diary."

I came across an old invitation for a reception celebrating the twenty-fifth anniversary of Lydia and Joseph Doolin—it would begin at 7:00 p.m. at their home at 610 John Street. I remember that, when I innocently asked my Aunt Lydia why the event was so late, she reminded me that for the Black people who worked in white peoples' homes, like most did, our plans for such celebrations were often delayed until "we got off work." Even Christmas dinner with our own families had to wait as we prepared and served someone else's meal. She recalled, "Had to get up at dawn, catch a ride to the Claytons, make their baked duck with orange sauce, potatoes, green beans, pies, cakes, Jell-O molds, dinner rolls, then get back home to make our own turkey and dressing, chitterlings, collard greens, strawberry cake, and sweet potato pie."

It was a long day, and it's easy to get angry when thinking about how exhausted our women must have been on the days they should have been enjoying their families. But they still took the time to feed us an unforgettable spread. That's love, and that makes the memories of those sweet potato pies just a little bit sweeter.

For nearly fifty years, both Lydia (1902–1975) and Joseph Doolin (1889–1970) worked for the Claytons, one of Hannibal's most prominent white families. Lydia was the maid and cook, and Joe was the chauffeur and houseman. The 1940 US Census lists Joe as a porter for the Claytons. Annually, he earned $624, while Lydia earned $364.

Joseph Doolin's 1925 chauffeur's license. He and his wife Lydia were both employed by a very prominent family, George D. Clayton and wife Mildred, who lived at #9 Stillwell Place. Their successful businesses included the Clayton Building and Loan, which remained in operation until the late twentieth century. An important leader in the community, Clayton served on the board of several major community organizations, including the Home Savings and Loan Association, Levering Hospital, the Free Public Library, Hannibal Railway Company and the Retail Merchants' Association.

OPPORTUNITIES GALORE: SEVENTY-TWO COOKS AND NINETY JANITORS

The 1927 Colored Directory lists seventy-two African American cooks and caterers in the area who would have worked in both private homes and restaurants. For decades,

Uniformed Lydia Dant Doolin headed to work for the Claytons.

Black people, including my mother, Arnetta, and my mother-in-law, Roxie Kelley Dant, would cook and clean in cafes and restaurants all over town, but they were never welcome to come in the front door and have a meal with dignity. Roxie died in 1960 before the passage of the Civil Rights Act of 1964, which ended segregation in public places, allowing her descendants to come and go in any restaurant they could afford. Like many Blacks of that era, even after desegregation, Roxie's husband, Melvin, was never keen on eating in restaurants that had previously refused to seat them.

1950s photograph of Vincton Frazier surrounded by loving family members. Photo courtesy of Marjorie Frazier.

Vincton Frazier (1898–1969) was the chef at the Mark Twain Hotel. He was husband to Maddie Nearing Frazier (1904–1984), and together, they had nine children who they raised at 822 North Street. The Mark Twain was one of Hannibal's most prestigious establishments. Built in 1905 with an upscale restaurant serving Hannibal's then booming population, it was one of the earliest establishments in town to cash in on the author's name. Dignitaries—including Samuel Clemens himself—stayed there when they visited. I asked my friend and another Douglasville resident, Robert "Bob" Frazier, to tell me about someone he admired, and he came up with his grandfather, Vincton.

"My grandfather likely had a hand in getting many Black residents their first job, including me," Bob recalled. "I started out at the Mark Twain Hotel at one dollar a

Roxie Kelley Dant (1911–1960). She was the cook at Renie's Cafe in the 1950s when this photograph was taken.

night, plus tips. I am proud of the fact that, within my first year, I had negotiated that up to three dollars a night. Hotel owner, Mr. Wilson, told me that, 'You won't get it if you don't ask for it." Bob was a high school student and this was his first job.

Bob remembers, "I really liked that job. It gave me an opportunity to be around my grandfather and experience some of his awesome food. I always signed up to work on Sunday. Brunch was the best—shrimp cocktail, roast beef and fried chicken, lamb chops, and scalloped oysters and desserts galore. Quite a change from my usual fare: Abe's tenderloins and Leon's pizza."

Bob is one of Douglasville's most accomplished kids of the sixties. He excelled in everything he tried—academics, sports, politics, girls, and business. Married with two children, he is now retired and living the best life in the state of Washington.

The 1927 Colored Directory also lists ninety janitors, a job with a mop and broom. But there is dignity in all work, and any cleaning of a public place was left to one of these ninety people. William Flanigan (1861–1927) is remembered in the 1927 directory as "one of our leading citizens." He cleaned the post office for forty years. My friend Richard Taylor (1923–2017) worked at Northeast Power in Palmyra, Missouri, for twenty-five years. He enjoyed mowing lawns and even had his own business. Richard was still the cleanup man for JC Penney when he was in his mid-eighties, and by then, his wife would be by his side. Soon after retirement, he and his wife, Rosa Ford Taylor (1924–2018), moved into Beth Haven Nursing Home.

Rosa was really my friend—a beautiful, kind smart lady. She and I would talk for hours—another community historian. She told me about her parents, Nathan and Fannie Macer Ford. Her father had been born in Kansas but died in Missouri, and he came from parents who had been enslaved in Missouri. "He often said that he hated that

Melvin Abbey (1926-1951). See the tools of his trade, a mop and bucket. Melvin is the son of Humphrey and Anna Abbey, who had six other children: Richard, Richard, Owen, Clara Bell, Muruell, and Velma.

he had to live in a state where his folks had been enslaved." Rosa raised her son, James Ford, in the house where my grandparents had raised their children, 202 Olive Street. I learned from them that it was not the "big" house I had imagined it to be.

Frank Green, my uncle, was another one of Hannibal's hardworking janitors. He was over eighty years old when he retired from Independent's Service Company. I remember him as a jokester who was always sporting a cigar or a cigarette. He was very civic-minded but knew how to have a good time, and he hosted card parties at his home at 415 North Ninth Street, with plenty of food and liquor (I heard). He and my aunt Julia Ely Green (1915–1996) were married for more than fifty years. Promising to always be by his side, she died on January 8, 1996, after his death on December 27, 1995—a promise kept.

Frank Green (1904-1995) and July Ely Green (1915-1996).

Chapter 4

FRIENDS, FAMILY, NEIGHBORS

Growing up in Hannibal, living with Colored friends, families, and neighbors was an awesome experience. Many of us refer to the fifties and sixties as "the good old days," where we knew all the Colored businesses, schools, churches, and neighborhoods. On the flip side, there were definitely some not-so-good days. There were all-white places and people we avoided. If you found yourself on the South Side or in Oakwood, you were sure to encounter problems. Personally, I avoided the little neighborhood grocer on Pleasant Street. The old biddy who ran it referred to us as "pickaninnies," watched our every move, and insisted that we put our money on the counter, ensuring that our fingers never touched hers.

Fortunately, Hannibal had a number of welcoming Black neighborhoods. I can recall Douglasville, the Westside, the Bottoms, Happy Hollow, Williamsville, Hoggs Row—there may have been more—where Black families settled and where they even built and owned their own homes.

Whether they grew up playing in the knee-high mud of the Bottoms or on the carefully kept lawns of the Westside, Black families in Hannibal relied on each other almost exclusively. It was a time when the only mixing of races happened for our parents when they went to work, or when we encountered the mailman or insurance man. Funny how that worked. For years we lived in an all-Black neighborhood, went to an all-Black school, and went to an all-Black church (when we went).

I had a white classmate tell me that he still remembers the day school opened in September of 1959, after integration: "I thought, where did all these Black kids come from?" he said.

DOUGLASVILLE AIN'T JUST A PLACE / *Rock Street, North Street, Ninth Street, and Hill Street*

Douglasville was way more than a neighborhood.

I loved Douglasville. It was a perfect place for a little Black girl growing up in the segregated fifties. There, I was surrounded by hardworking people who were committed to making a way out of no way in response to barriers that were both visible and invisible. I thrived in this mostly self-sufficient neighborhood, where we found sanctuary from legalized segregation. As a kid, experience had taught me that white people were to be avoided. Straying even a block out of the neighborhood often meant taunting, rock-throwing, name-calling, and bloody noses.

In recent years, I have learned that Douglasville was Hannibal's oldest Black neighborhood. Post-Emancipation, it prospered despite segregation. And by the early thirties, it sported some of our most prominent citizens and community leaders. It was also the site of our oldest school, our oldest church, our oldest Black-owned businesses and early entrepreneurs—many newly freed and hopeful.

The "most undesirable" plots Joe Douglas (1821–1923) had purchased all those many years ago meant the landscape was never easy to maneuver—our streets were all hills, only good for sledding or racing homemade go-carts down. Here, we all knew our adult neighbors and all the children on both sides of the street, including cousins who became our first best friends. Many businesses moved in and out for decades: grocery stores, restaurants, transfer companies, and even a gas station.

Our humble wood-frame houses lined dirt roads, all rocks and gravel. Not easy on foot or in a car. The streets were not paved until well into the sixties, sometime after many of the old wood-framed homes had fallen down or were demolished. Our homes were replaced with new subsidized housing, and white people moved in and changed the color of Douglasville forever. Even the new little city park is named for a dead white woman nobody knows: Dorsey Park.

I was born in the spring of 1949, and Mom brought me home to our house at 923 Rock Street, at the foot of the hill. We had a living room with a kitchenette, a bedroom, and a half bath (adults and children took baths in a tin tub). We lived here for just a few years.

We then moved up the hill to 1105c Rock Street. It was a very nice apartment with a big yard and a big front porch. We were able to move into one of the three units built for recently returning World War II veterans. I'm proud to say that I was raised in one of Hannibal's first federal housing units—the Projects.

Zella Ruth Riding with her sister Laura Hood. Zella was another neighbor and played every day with Gregory and Toni. They lived at 1105B Rock Street.

I remember this home very well. We had two bedrooms, a living room, a kitchen, and a bathroom with a shower. My mom and stepfather had a bedroom, the boys shared a bedroom, and I slept on a rollaway in the living room. Besides not having any privacy, I hated being awakened every Saturday morning by that noisy old wringer-style washing machine, mostly because it signaled the beginning of family cleaning day. Let me say, you have to be taught how to clean—and we were, me and my brothers.

Saturday afternoon and evening were different. The living room filled up with friends, and the kitchen turned into Arnetta's Beauty Parlor. Colored women and girls from all over town came to get their hair fixed—a hot press and curl. For many Black women born with kinky hair, and for women needing to generate some extra income, the kitchen was not just a place where food was cooked and served, it was the place where our hair was "fried" and straightened with the dreaded hot comb. This was such a frequent occurrence in many homes that we coined the phrase "kitchen hairdresser." And like any real hair salon, there was a lot of advice being dished out, a lot of gossiping, and a lot of laughing. I suppose that with Mom being the oldest girl in a family with five younger sisters, she had plenty of practice.

While I didn't think much about it, we were poor, like most of our neighbors. My mom cleaned houses, and my stepfather worked as a laborer. Luckily, Mom was an awesome cook. We ate a lot of soul food: beans and cornbread, greens, neck bones, everything on the hog—ears, feet, and tails—buffalo fish, carp, and catfish from the Mississippi, and wild game—rabbits, squirrels, and raccoons. Greens were a mainstay, and we often went foraging with Mom in the nearby woods, where we found dandelions, crow's feet, dock, lamb's quarters, black mustard, and poke. We also raised chickens and rabbits. I can still see Mom wringing a chicken's neck for Sunday dinner. We ate it all, including the feet. Holiday meals, of course, were very special, with homemade rolls and cobblers.

We wore mostly hand-me-down clothes, had used furniture and a used car, and we never owned a bike or a sled. Our friend Butch King had both. He generously shared and gave us those things he tired of or outgrew. My favorite toy was cut-out paper dolls from a Sears catalog and an old shoebox for a dollhouse. I loved it—It meant hours of fun away from the boys. I also read a lot, grew up on *Little Women* and *The Bobbsey Twins* as well as *Jet* and *Ebony*.

We played outside all year and explored every inch of the neighborhood with pure abandon. There were kids everywhere; it seemed like every family had at least four or five children. In fact, the Haleys had ten, the Fraziers had eleven, and the Simons outpaced everyone with twenty-five (the father, Frank Simon, had two wives), though I must admit I only learned this from the recent obituary for GoldieMae Simon, another sharp Douglasville lady.

GoldieMae Simon, center.

We played hard, but the truth is we spent a lot more time working. We were very enterprising, constantly trying to earn money for one thing or another. Our favorite treats included grapes from Goochies or the A&P, candy or soda pop from Tinsley's, carnival rides, show tickets, fireworks, or even new canvas shoes for the September start of school. We babysat, shoveled snow, and cut grass; we collected and sold pop bottles; we sold grit; and we even made and sold pot holders. Most often, though, we'd get up extra early and head to our favorite spot in the neighboring woods to hunt for fishing worms. It wasn't easy work, fighting off bugs and turning over heavy rocks to find the elusive family of earthworms, but finding them was just the beginning. We had to hawk those worms at a nickel a piece to fishermen near and far. We always sold out and never came home empty-handed.

Needless to say, summer was our favorite time of year. We were always outside playing, scantily dressed and barefoot. Our favorite activities included tag, hide-and-go-seek, and sock ball. We turned a fallen tree into a ship or explored an abandoned house or even scared up some bees to chase us back inside. And if it was hot enough, we'd get sprayed with the hose! We spent many summer evenings out on the porch (we had no air-conditioning), eating stove-popped popcorn and drinking Kool-Aid. Grown folks always built a rag fire to run mosquitoes away while some shared a jug or two of beer from Fouche's at the Wedge. The ten-o-clock whistle usually signaled that it was time to go in.

In September of 1959, I started the fifth grade at Pettibone School, five blocks from where my family lived. I knew I was leaving Douglass School, where my family had attended for generations, to go here. Oddly enough, the only thing I remember about the new white school was the loneliness. There were no other Black kids in my class, and there were no Black teachers. The bell ringing at the end of the school day was what I longed for the most.

One of my happiest memories of Douglasville was when my cousins—five girls and one boy—moved into an apartment in the three-unit complex. My first best friend, Cousin Jeanie, was finally close enough that we could see each other and play together every day. She was sweet and smart and pretty, with beautiful thick hair, and very responsible. We were about the same age, and we quickly became inseparable. Being the only girl in a family with four rough-and-ready boys, I was more spoiled. But Jeanie, who was the oldest of her seven siblings, was often responsible for their care: changing diapers, feeding them, and putting them to bed. We were best friends until life took us in different directions. Jeanie fell in love, moved from Hannibal, and had two beautiful daughters (Kendra and Bobbie). I stuck around long enough to receive a degree from our two-year college, married a hometown guy, and landed in Michigan. While Jeanie and I went separate ways, always hundreds of miles apart, we stayed best friends all our life, exchanging advice and loving each other until her death from breast cancer in 2005.

I loved Douglasville. Despite our very humble beginnings, some of the children from the neighborhood became CEOs, CFOs, attorneys, doctors, entrepreneurs, authors, scientists, and ministers. Some of them became pimps and criminals. It was a close-knit community, and the people there took great pride in it and formed lifelong relationships—a few even married each other. The Colliers, Smiths, Andersons, Farrises, Fraziers, Greens, Andersons, Haleys, Conleys, Elys, Tinsleys, Dorseys, Letchers, Beals, Brights, Browns, and Simons—all families who raised Douglasville kids like me.

Peter F. Dealy (1862–1950) was from the second generation of emancipated Douglasville residents. His parents, Frank Dealy (1826–1905) and Emily (1836–1921), had two other children, James and Mildred. Frank, by the way, was a Civil War veteran—his probated will left Peter

Unidentified neighbors standing at the door of the P. F. Dealy Grocery at 408 North Ninth.

this property when he died. Peter is identified as a grocer as early as 1920 until the 1940s. He was married to Susie Blackwell; she and a son lived in Springfield, Illinois, where Peter later died. I discovered an interesting record for Peter in the 1891 US Register of Federal Employees; he is listed with nine other mail carriers. Hannibal had ten total—all of whom were white (except for Peter) and were earning $850 a year. Peter earned $1 a year. Reparations time!

THE BOTTOMS / Lemon, Wardlow, Collier, E. Gordon, Vermont, Munger, and Fifteenth Streets

I reached out to Lilly Divers King Jackson, one of the smartest, most levelheaded, humble women I know. Mrs. Jackson is a ninety-one-year-old widow with zero memory loss, and she is full of wisdom. I call her a community historian, she calls herself a clipper. She recently declined my request for an article she had once told me about. The article is of course "put away." I smiled when she said, "It's not the getting it out, it's the putting it back."

When I asked her to tell me about life in Hannibal, she began: "I was born in Columbia, came to Hannibal in 1948, married King, and we had JimEd in 1949." James "JimEd" King was my classmate, and he died in 2005. She made it clear to me that their home at 1275 Collier was not in the Bottoms—they lived above the tracks, and the Bottoms were below the tracks. This is where she raised her ten children. For years, she mainly did day work, and because she didn't drive a car until later in life, she walked everywhere. Her daughter Vonna taught her to drive when she was in her thirties. She worked for old George Riedel—"the one y'all always asking for money," was how she described him (he's founder of the Riedel Foundation)—and took care of him until he died in 2000. She refused to share any of their family secrets with me. Of course, we

A footrace in Douglasville—Walter Haley is in the lead, followed by Stanley Clark and Steve Letcher. In the background are the homes of Rev. Isaac Haley and Frank and Julia Green. (The Green home still stands in 2019.) Credit: Photograph by Bill Ray, Missouri Photo Workshop.

Unidentified, very proud individuals posing with their dog near the intersection of North Ninth and Rock Street in the 1930s. I recognize the house on the hill. It belonged to Miss Pinkie. She was a lovely lady, very nice to children and dogs. She was always good for a nickel.

talked about how it used to be and how "no matter what your status was, Black folks had the good sense to speak to each other."

We agreed on the importance of knowing your history, especially local history.

"Hannibal's had a lot going on," she said. Yes, there were a lot of Black businesses. Her father-in-law purchased the house she currently lives in with earnings from his barbershop, King's Barbershop and Pool Hall on Main Street. We had some big-time entertainers come through before they got real big: Ike and Tina Turner, Ray Charles, B. B. King, Cab Calloway, and Bill Doggett. In fact, Bill Doggett stayed in the Bottoms, right there in the Blakeys' house, when he performed here. When they played at either Hales Skating Rink or the Armory, tickets were only about two dollars. Mrs. Jackson said, "I never heard anyone, I didn't go out to the joints." When I asked her for the names of families who lived in the Bottoms, she not only knew their names—the Buckners, the Porters, the Deans, Harry Britts, Broadus, LaJoy, Hall, the McElroys, Allison, Stanton, Moore, and on and on—she also knew the streets they lived on. She also told me that her mother, Anna Divers, and her uncle grew up in Douglasville. It was an awesome conversation, though this was only the information she wanted on the record. We chatted and laughed for well over an hour before I hung up.

First row: Stanley Clark, Alecia Jones, Jeanie Farris, Joe Dixon, Martha Jackson, Choteau Simon, Mike Davis, Floyd Jackson, and me, Faye Dant. The big kids in the back are Joe Dixon, Margaret Ann Cassidy, Addie Frazier, and Sue Dixon. We're all dressed pretty cute—must be a Sunday.

All the businesses in the area were gone by the late sixties. This meant the end of the venues that welcomed our early Black entertainers and gave them a place to eat, sleep, work, and perform. Playing the Chitlin Circuit meant that Black entertainers made a living traveling all over to find a Black-owned restaurant or joint where they could perform and have a meal with dignity, or a private home they could sleep in. These Black entertainers also performed for white audiences, and it was just that. A friend told me a story about Count Basie performing at the Casino—a pretty upscale Quincy venue. Blacks that wanted to see him were escorted to the basement of the theater, where Basie knowingly went to find them during intermission. He shook a few hands before going back upstairs.

Black residents were only allowed to build, purchase a house, or live in the less desirable areas, like the Bottoms. A vibrant Black community that grew up from the soggy ground of this area, where the waters of Bear Creek were always dangerously close, forever threatening to overflow its banks.

Over time, the houses were torn down, too. The community lives on in the memories of its former residents. Eventually, people were not allowed to rebuild in the floodplain of Bear Creek, and they were forced to sell their homes to make way for the new wastewater

The home at 600 Fifteenth Street, maintained by generations of McElroys.

treatment plant. Shirley Stanton Allison tells me that her mother, Laura Eugene Stanton, was one of the first residents to move out.

When Valerie Hawkins Shaw thinks of growing up in Hannibal, she thinks of her family's magnificent home in the Bottoms—more than the floods. The home was built by her great-grandfather Henry Clay McElroy (1850–1925) around 1900. Valerie's grandparents Charles (1879–1954) and Elizabeth "Muddy" (1887–1987) Frazier moved in the day they married in 1901.

Valerie's mother, Lillian McElroy Hawkins Jones (1928–2019), was one of eight children, all raised in this lovely home. It was not only the biggest house on the block, but it was also one of the largest Black-owned homes in Hannibal. It had a big porch, big yard, big garden, and a big hardworking family. There were five bedrooms, a summer kitchen, indoor plumbing, an attached apartment, and a space the family used for a restaurant. They raised everything they needed in their garden, and they had rabbits and a yard full of chickens.

"And the smells!" she remembers. "With a house full of cooks and bakers, the aromas were overwhelming."

"Don't know how we managed," she goes on. "We always had a full house. I can remember Mom telling me that three Douglass School students from Monroe City—Lois, Bette, and Frances Buckner—boarded here while attending school."

The Blakeys' house at 3 Myers Row, a neighborhood grocery store. It was owned by James Blakey (1887–1918) and his wife Lutie (1898–1978). James was a tailor, and Lutie ran the store. Their son James Jr. (1914–1995) was a barber at the Wedge. They also let rooms to the entertainers who came to town. It took a lot of work to build this small house.

It was a family home in every sense. When one relative moved out, another moved in. Many worked in the family's hot tamale business, serving and delivering tamales all over town. At the helm of it all was Granny—the matriarch—a formidable baker who occasionally worked for a fancy local restaurant.

"My grandmother was a treasure," Valerie said. "She was so kind and showed all of her family absolute and unconditional love."

Chester Brown (1905–1981) and his wife, Florine (1908–1983), owned Brown's Tavern on Lemon Street. He was likely able to purchase the bar because he also worked many years at the Rubber Plant. Cliff Burton's Tavern was at 1322 East Gordon Street. Clifford Burton (1898–1989) was married to Chrysolia Burton (1916–1968). Through the years, the bars had various owners and numerous name changes. Eventually, they were all demolished. The regular flooding of Bear Creek likely contributed. Near the Colored joints, Myers Row was one of many informal safe havens for Blacks who needed a place to buy groceries, get a meal, or get a haircut. Myers Row could also be dangerous, and it had a record of fatal shootings and stabbings. Joel Dant recounted how his Uncle Jerome Dant (1907–1934) was murdered there on the evening his mother and father were married.

Jerome is in the middle at the head of the table and, yes, very good looking. Melvin Dant is on the right. Taken in 1930, it's a group of Black Lodge members taken on Myers Row.

Jackie Stanton (center), his sister, Shirley, and an unidentified friend in the Bottoms in the 1960s. In the background is their home at 702 Vermont.

Gordon Street kids Kevin Bruce Taylor and his friend, Keisha Duncan. Neither looked very happy about having to hold hands for the picture. Look closely and you will see some of the beautifully well-kept homes and lawns in the background.

Jerome was just twenty-six years old—"we've been told that there was a woman involved and the murderer never spent a day in jail," Joel remembers.

WESTSIDE / Chestnut, Gordon, Hayden, Hope, Lamb, Richmond, Settles, Spruce, and Willow Streets

The Westside is where many of Hannibal's most accomplished Blacks lived. It was also a rare neighborhood where Blacks and whites lived side by side for many years. Unlike Douglasville or the Bottoms, there were more single-family, two-story homes—and no steep inclines or the threat of floods. Douglass School, the pride of Hannibal's Black community, was on the Westside as well. This naturally meant more schoolteachers and administrators lived here.

Minnie Morrison Smith was born, grew up, married, and lived here with her husband, Phil Smith, and they raised their two sons, Marcus and Anson. Minnie spent her childhood in communion with others, so it was no surprise that she'd become a pastor one day. Pastor Minnie recently retired from Willow Street Christian Church.

Smith recalled the first house she grew up in, the same house where she and her brother William Jr. were born more than eighty years ago. She has some wonderful memories of her first home, 2105 Spruce Street. It was owned by Wallace (1860–?) and Sarah Dixon (no relation to the Palmyra Dixons). "There were about twelve rooms in the two-story house, and it was beautifully decorated. I knew they were special because they had a live-in housekeeper and butler," Smith said. "Black people were locked out of public accommodations, so the house often seemed more like a hotel or restaurant."

Smith remembered Wallace as a retired railroad man, very quiet, who "I often found peeling apples, which

Pick-up softball game on the Douglass School playground. The homes in the background are on Gordon Street.

Brothers Anthony and William "Billy" Cotton with their pet hound dog and a litter of pups at 1917 Settles Street.

he would gladly share with me." Sarah was a homemaker, and daughter Thelma was a Douglass School teacher.

The couple were documented with roots in Hannibal as early as 1909. It is unclear what year Wallace and Sarah purchased the house at 2105 Spruce. But in 1939, that's where Minnie Morrison entered the world.

"My parents (both 1936 Douglass School graduates), Lucille Moore Morrison (1918–2003) and William Morrison (1917–1991), lived here in a two-room apartment. My father was a cook for the Wallaces; he started right after he graduated high school. I considered the whole house mine," Smith said, "And I often refer to their housekeeper, Jennie Smith, as my nanny. She was a small, almost frail older lady. When my parents went to work, she was always there for me and my older brother, Billy."

From the beginning, Minnie and her brother, William Morrison Jr., grew up surrounded by loved ones: one set of grandparents in the Bottoms, another on the Westside, and aunts and uncles in Douglasville. Both sets of parents had lived here for generations. And we recently found the Old Baptist Cemetery tombstone of her great-great-uncle, William Morrison, a Civil War veteran—United States Colored Troops.

"I was very proud to attend a ceremony installing a memorial for him and other Civil War soldiers at the entrance to the cemetery," Smith said.

The house at 2105 Spruce was always abuzz with visitors having a good time. There was card playing, drinking, good food, and lots of laughter. Most memories Smith spoke of were about growing up on Hannibal's Westside, less than a mile from Douglass School. She understood that her neighborhood was considered "upper-crust," and she smiled when she learned that some even referred to her street as "Cherry Lane."

"I don't know why, maybe it was because so many white people still lived on the street," she speculates. "Because for me it was a neighborhood of working-class families. Some homeowners, some renters, and some boarders. In fact, I only remember two people owning cars."

Minnie didn't know whether to be happy or not as change came.

"I can remember when the Dixons moved to California to be near their daughter," she recalled. Thelma had married and lived with her husband in LA—her aging parents moved in with her, and both died there.

"But not before he helped my father get a job on the railroad," Minnie continues. "My father rose to become head chef responsible for feeding traveling dignitaries as they traveled all over the country. It meant he was gone a lot, but we were well taken care of."

The integration of Hannibal's schools brought more changes—the last Douglass School graduation was in 1954. As a sophomore, Minnie transitioned to Hannibal High School from Douglass, and she soon recognized how under-resourced Douglass had been. Despite this fact, she and many of her Douglass classmates were well prepared, as it didn't take long for her and many of her classmates to qualify for the National Honor Society. Many of the boys also excelled in sports.

"Not all of my Douglass classmates showed up on that first day of school at Hannibal High," Minnie recalled. "I heard it was because they felt their clothes weren't good enough. It was too bad and sad because they had loved school."

Soon after graduation, Minnie married her high school sweetheart, Phil Smith. The couple purchased their first home where they raised their two sons, Marcus and Anson, at 2677 Spruce. After her sons were raised, Minnie went to college and got her bachelor's degree. She was a longtime professional with thirty-eight years working for the Social Security Administration. After retirement, she started working as one of the pastors of her family church, Willow Street Christian Church. Early on she focused her ministry on the many at-risk and economically disadvantaged children in the neighborhood, and beyond. Two of her proudest moments include managing a successful after-school tutoring program, Caring Hands, and convincing the city to memorialize the Wedge, Hannibal's earliest Black business district, with a five-foot tall bronze plaque on its site. Her husband, Phil, a longtime Hannibal resident, a Douglass graduate, and a US Army veteran, ended up going to college across the river, in Quincy, Illinois. He enjoyed a highly successful career at Blessing Hospital and retired as director of ancillary laboratory services for Quincy's Blessing Hospital.

In 2015, Minnie was ordained as a minister in the Willow Street Christian Church, the original Disciples of Christ church that was built on Broadway in 1870.

HAPPY HOLLOW / South Section, Gerard, Center, Olive, and Maple Avenue

Many of Hannibal's Black neighborhoods were no more than a street or two where just enough Black people lived to feel safe. It included South Section Street, where Bonnie and George L. Green and Mattie Ford lived. Dr. Welch lived on Center Street. Girard Street had Chote and Grace Fouche and the Colored American Legion. And Mr. Brooks and his auntie were teachers at Douglass High School. Mr. and Mrs. Maceo Wilson and my grandparents lived on Olive Street.

The urban renewal projects of later years changed that forever.

A lovely fourplex that once stood on Maple Avenue. Four families were displaced when this building was torn down.

Alfred Johnson (1945–2014) in the late 1950s. He's easily recognized because he was one of the few Black kids who owned a bicycle. Alfred knew when he got the bike that it likely meant sharing with his friends. His passion for speed continued when he later became the proud owner of a Corvette.

Mattie Ford Willis (1914–1988) enjoys her 206 North Section Street home in the 1950s. The baby she's holding is likely her grandson Craig. Mattie is best described as an enterprising woman who for decades owned and operated businesses at the Wedge and in the Bottoms. Mattie's Paradise Bar and Grill was one very popular spot for good food and fun. She employed many hardworking Black residents. Sherry Farris Cannon remembered that her mother, Mendill Farris, was one of Mattie's most dedicated barmaids—Sherry smiles when she talks about how she would show up at the bar as a fifteen-year-old, seeking dinner money, and often find herself slinging beer to patrons during happy hour.

FREE TO ROAM IN THE COUNTRY

Celia Thompson and her young daughter moved here to Hannibal fifteen years ago from Pembroke, Illinois. She has truly embraced our community, working, volunteering, and fully engaged. Celia has her own story to tell.

Pembroke, Illinois, was founded by Pap Tetter, who escaped enslavement before the Emancipation Proclamation. Folk history tells us that he and his family of eighteen children fled North Carolina around 1861. After the Civil War, other freed slaves arrived and also bought land here—land that nobody else wanted—very sandy soil, not good for much. They thought.

Pembroke ended up with one of the largest concentrations of Black farmers north of the Mason-Dixon Line.

"We invested our blood, sweat, and tears into the land on farms where we raised crops and cattle," Celia said. "It was a loving community for me growing up. We bartered for eggs, chickens, and anything else that kept us out of the grocery store. My fondest memory is of our all-Black community, the school and churches. It was a community and a time where kids had to be involved in either school or sports, church activities, performing in a play or joining the choir or serving as an usher, or junior usher. I learned to love it. There were eight of us in my family, four boys and four girls. While it has changed a lot, I can't deny that I'm a country girl and I still love to get 'home' as often as I can."

After Emancipation, many people who had once been forced to work on the farm as slaves and sharecroppers craved to get their own land to cultivate. In the late 1800s and early 1900s, many scrimped and saved to buy a piece of land. The more things change, the more things stay the same—not much of the land we were able to purchase was very valuable, it was generally not tillable, and the trees we cleared were worthless. But it was ours.

The Dants were part of this group of "born-to-farm" people and landowners. One of them, Joel Dant, loves the country. Joel's father, Melvin Dant Sr., and grandfather, Charles Dant, loved the country too. So did his formerly enslaved great-grandfather, William Henry Dant, who played his fiddle and sold brooms so he could purchase his own farm.

When most other Black families were moving to the city, Melvin Dant Sr. chose to leave town and move back to the country with his wife Roxie. Roxie Kelly Dant, was a country girl, daughter of Truman Kelly (1883–1958) and Cora Stewart (1891–1955).

Joel returned to back this sixty-plus-acre family farm in 2011. When he did, he reclaimed the title as one of the largest Black landowners in Ralls County.

The Dant farm, a scenic piece of land on the outskirts of Hannibal, is the setting for many fond memories. Looking out the picture window of the house, Joel can easily imagine the red glow of a cigarette casting the shadow of his mother as she snuck a smoke in the outhouse. Pop would be sitting in his easy chair, listening to the Cardinals play over the radio. Joel and his brother Melvin would be in bed; they had to get up at dawn to do their chores before school—gather eggs and milk the cows.

They purchased the seventy acres just off New London Gravel Road for $2,000 in 1949. "I don't know how my folks did it, my dad on a janitor's salary, and mother as a cleaning lady in several homes and cooking in local restaurants," recalls Joel.

"Our dad didn't believe in letting people sleep in," Melvin added with a chuckle. "We had the farm and always had work to do, but we also did have a lot of fun exploring the woods around us. I learned to hunt at an early age—we'd often bring home a rabbit or a squirrel, both made a great meal. Every day in the country was an adventure for me and Joel."

He added, with a hint of sarcasm in his voice, "we never found any Tom and Huck stuff. No bodies and no caves."

Experience in Jim Crow Hannibal? "I tried eating out but was asked on several occasions to leave local restaurants," Joel remembered. "I was with my white 'friends' and naive enough to think that I would be served along with them. Sadly, my mother had worked in several of these restaurants over the years but died of cancer in 1960, never able to legally sit down with her family and enjoy a meal in one. Because of this, my father was never too keen on restaurant meals."

Joel added another warning that his father gave to him: "Get out of Hannibal. No matter your qualifications, they'll only hand you a broom."

Unlike most Blacks, the Dants know a lot about their ancestors' lives: Joe and Sue Dant were enslaved people

Uncle Joseph Lee Dant (1871–1955) and his wife, Mary Frances Woods Dant (1868–1945). Joseph is the son of the formerly enslaved William Henry Dant. He is identified as a farmer living in South River Township when he died. It is believed that the white women in this photograph were their employers, and could be descendants of their former enslavers. Like many in the first generation of free Black people, they often went to work on the farms where their parents and grandparents had been enslaved.

Roxie Kelly Dant (back right) poses with relatives.

brought to Missouri from Kentucky. Their son, William Henry Dant—Joel and Melvin's great-grandfather—was born enslaved in northeastern Missouri, as was his son Charles. Post-Emancipation, the Dants worked as farmhands but soon moved on to purchase their own land.

"Dad never finished high school," Melvin recalled, "but in retrospect, he was probably one of the smartest people I knew. He learned how to manage his money. His dream was to own his own farm, and he accomplished that."

"Dad wanted to have something to leave us as a legacy. When he and my mother bought the farm," Joel said. "It wasn't easy. Those were dangerous times for Blacks in rural Missouri."

The original house had three rooms, a coal stove, and no indoor plumbing. At dawn, the Dant boys would have to get up extra early to do their chores before heading to school. "I bet I smelt like the cow manure on my boots and smoke from that stove in the middle of the living room," Joel said, grinning. Melvin, ribbing his brother, recalled having to milk Joel's cows because Joel, who was three years younger, couldn't keep up.

"Sometimes there were five or six of us gathered in that little three-room house," Melvin remembered. "My older sister, Charlotte (we call her Bobbie), lived in town, but her three children, our contemporaries, also loved the country and spent every free moment with us. We had a ball. It was fun, and we didn't know how poor we were."

It was a working farm in every sense, and the Dants didn't need much from the local grocer—they had cattle, hogs, and chickens. They grew hay and corn for their livestock, and they had a two-acre garden where they grew beans, tomatoes, greens, and other vegetables; Melvin remembers a whole half-acre just for potatoes—"what we didn't eat or sell, Mom canned." They milked their cows and even made their own butter. For spending money, the boys would go door to door, selling eggs and vegetables in town. The family butchered several hogs each year and sold the meat but always shared some with family. The Dant boys' childhood came with all the trappings of life on the farm. Joel and Melvin were the first Black members of the Ralls County 4H. "It saddened me to see my calf, Belle, show up on our dinner table one evening," Melvin said.

"The country was an awesome way to grow up," Joel recalled. "But it was not without its pitfalls. Early on we did have some livestock killed and never found out what really happened, leaving little doubt that an unfriendly neighbor was responsible. We knew they existed, just based on the number of rocks we had to duck on those treks through their Oakwood neighborhood when walking to and from town."

For the first few years of schooling, Joel and his brother were driven to the all-Black Douglass School in town—the rural schools were still segregated at the time. In 1955 after the *Brown v. Board of Education of Topeka* decision, the Dant boys began attending Ocean

Wave School, a one-room schoolhouse near the farm. Another first: They were the school's first Black students.

"We knew we were going to have issues early on," Joel said. One morning, the boys arrived at school to find a rifle placed across their teacher's desk. On the blackboard were the crudely written words, "KILL ALL NIGGERS." Melvin remembered their teacher, Daisy Smith, calling the authorities and a meeting of the PTA. "Even she knew it was wrong," he said.

"I really thought someone meant to kill us," Joel said. After telling Pop about the incident, he took to carrying a gun to all school gatherings.

Despite the tensions of integration, the Dant family made a place for themselves among some of their white neighbors: they sometimes even borrowed each other's farm equipment. "My dad always got called when other farmers needed to castrate calves," Joel said. "I guess it was because he was so big and strong. Once a year, in the fall, we butchered our own hogs." This was referred to as "hog killin' day," and it always conjures up fond memories.

"We had a little smokehouse where we cured and kept the cured meat to eat on all winter," Joel said. "Silly me, I would trade my cured ham sandwiches for hot dogs."

Joel and Mel became close enough with one family up the road that they occasionally invited the boys over, where they gathered around their two-channel black-and-white TV to watch *Gunsmoke* or *Ed Sullivan*.

Joel was ten and Melvin thirteen when their little sister, Tysa, was born in 1958. She was a real cutie. Their mother, Roxie, got very sick soon after Tysa was born. She was

Roxie (1911-1960) and her daughter, Tysa, probably a Sunday at Aunt Ellabell's (1898-1968) home. Her beautiful mother is so happy to see her fifteen-month-old baby girl trying to walk. Despite the pain she must have been in, Roxie obviously loved this late-in-life surprise.

treated at the Ellis Fischel Cancer Hospital in Columbia, Missouri, the first cancer center west of the Mississippi River. Joel said, "Our older sister Bobbie was very involved in the care of our forty-eight-year-old mother, who died May 4, 1960, after a yearlong battle. Our baby sister, Tysa, went to live with Aunt Ellabelle, Pop's sister"

"It was just Pops and us guys for the next few years," Joel said. Then, once Melvin went away to college, it was just Joel. Mr. Dant remarried, this time to a former Douglass School teacher named Ruth Abbey. She was one of the few teachers who got a job at one of the white schools, Eugene Field. They moved to her home on Pine Street in town. "I loved it," Joel said. "She was an awesome stepmother and a way better cook than Pop." The fact is, Joel gained forty pounds the first year they lived with Ruth. Good cooking will do that to a young man.

"Farm living was an awesome way to grow up," Joel says. "But I sure liked taking a hot shower in my own bathroom!" The farm was still without indoor plumbing.

Joel graduated from Hannibal High School in 1966. He was recruited straight off the Douglass School basketball court and given a scholarship to play basketball for the local Hannibal LaGrange Junior College. He was good enough to get the attention of the basketball coach at Culver-Stockton College (thirty miles from home), where he received his bachelor's degree. Following in the footsteps of a lifelong family friend and one of his idols, Larry Thompson, Joel applied for the master's program at Michigan State. Armed with a master's degree in labor and industrial relations, he looked pretty good to the Ford Motor Company. Long story short, he became a highly successful human resources professional for more than forty years. He and I married, and we have three children (Joel, Kalecia, and Jenni) and three grandchildren (Redd, Journey, and Albert). In those forty-plus years, we've moved more than ten times: Michigan, Minnesota, and the Chicago suburbs before returning to Missouri in 2011.

Melvin Dant Jr. graduated from Hannibal High in 1962. He has the distinction of being the first Black elected vice president of his class at Hannibal-LaGrange College, a school that, not long before, had rejected the enrollment of Black students. He has a bachelor's degree from Kirksville Teachers College. He is a Vietnam War veteran and a retired sales professional. He lives in the Chicagoland area with Barbara, his wife of more than fifty years. They have two children and three grandchildren.

Chapter 5

LEARNING AGAINST ALL ODDS

Educated slaves posed a great threat to their white masters. An 1847 Missouri law made it illegal to teach a Black person, free or enslaved, to read and write. So it made sense that former slaves were hopeful that education was the great equalizer—it was all they needed to fit in, to attain success, to overcome racism. Nelson Mandela said, "Education is the most powerful weapon which you can use to change the world." And as Hannibal's own Lena Mason put it best in the title of one of her poems, "Educate a Negro and You No Longer Have a Slave." Even in a hostile Missouri.

In 1853, Hannibal's free Blacks opened Missouri's oldest "common," or "tuition," school, a private school in the African Church (now Eighth and Center Streets Missionary Baptist Church). Children and adults came there to learn. The one-room cabin was built by Rev. Oliver Webb (1823–1918), and the first teacher was a free Black man, James Henderson (1855–1925). Future senator Blanche Kelso Bruce (1841–1898) was another early teacher here. The church school closed just before the end of the Civil War, and Bruce left Missouri and went on to become a graduate of Oberlin College before he headed home to Mississippi. Here, he had an impressive political career. He became the first Black full-term senator and register of the treasury and has the distinction of being the only Black man with his name on US paper currency.

The first Hannibal public school for Colored children was the Douglasville School, located at 925 Rock Street (1870–1881), serving grades one through three. It had been mandated that if there were twenty or more Blacks in a community, then the community leaders had to open an elementary school. Overcrowding soon forced the opening of a second school, Lincoln School, on Fulton Avenue. After much protest, the Black families—most formerly enslaved and very suspicious—got their first Black teachers.

Mrs. Whaley, a Douglasville teacher, seems to be overseeing a game of Ring around the Rosie, with an unknown mother looking on. Mrs. Whaley brought the love and dedication these children in grades one through three needed. She had two sons, both Lincoln University graduates.

The Douglass School, which was built in response to the community's desire to have a school that went beyond the fourth grade.

Just fifteen years after Emancipation, Douglass School (named after the iconic abolitionist Frederick Douglass) was built at Barton and Willow (404 Willow Street). The school, originally an eight-room structure, was completed in 1885. It was a bond that gave the school board $8,856 to build the brick building for grades five through twelve. First through fifth grade classrooms were on the first floor and those for sixth through twelfth grade on the second floor. Most surrounding communities had elementary schools, but students wanting to learn beyond the fourth grade came here to Douglass. Joseph Pelham (1848–1928) arrived from Michigan. He was just twenty-six years old when he was hired as the new Colored school superintendent responsible for two branch schools—Douglasville and Lincoln—as well as the new Douglass School. The residents got much more than they anticipated. He was an outstanding educator and community leader, a notary, a property owner, and an insurance agent. Documents can be found with his stamp ensuring that former Civil War soldiers or their wives received the Civil War pensions promised to them. He married Jenny Pelham, and they had five children, all Douglass graduates.

Dozens of students came to Douglass High School from nearby communities: Frankford, New London, Canton, Palmyra, LaBelle, LaGrange, Hunnewell, Monroe City, Shelbina, and Shelbyville. Those districts provided transportation and paid $100 in tuition per student each year. Douglass "grew its own teachers" determined to educate their family, friends, and neighbors. The faculty and staff of the school did what they could with what little resources the Hannibal Public Schools system provided, filling in many of the gaps themselves. With the end of legalized segregation that September of 1955, our high school students (tenth, eleventh, and twelfth grade) transitioned to Hannibal High School. The elementary and middle schools were still in use when Douglass School closed in 1959. The city had built two new schools, including

Image of the Douglass School graduating class of 1955, the last students to graduate from there. Most of those students would be in their mid-eighties now. Row one: Shirley Douglas, Mona Williams, Mary Lucille McElroy, Rondell Lasley. Row two: Professor Thomas Miller, Cristola Wallace, Charlotte Woods, Velma Ward, and Principal C. C. Wells. Row three: Lois McBride, Charles Porter, Joe L. Frazier, Delbert Williams.

Hannibal Junior High School and Mark Twain Elementary School; both opened to receive Hannibal's first integrated classes. This ended segregated education for our feeder schools as well, but it didn't end racism. To be clear: Blacks were never clamoring to go to school with white children. We were clamoring for equal resources and services. Only three of our Douglass teachers were hired to teach in the newly integrated classrooms.

By the time Douglass School closed, it had graduated 679 students, and many went on to become the best citizens they could be. Over the years, many Douglass graduates moved away. Some went as far as working in the White House. Others stayed in Hannibal, determined to make Douglass proud.

I started first grade at the segregated Douglass School in 1955. I made some new friends there beyond my Douglasville gang. My family had attended Douglass for generations. It was all Black—students, teachers, and administrators. We had our own basketball and track teams as well as school patrol officers, cheerleaders, prom kings and queens, and a PTA. I especially loved my Brownie troop and the programs that were offered in the school auditorium. We had an awesome band and chorus, which included my brothers, cousins, aunts, and uncles. At Douglass, my Black teachers were Miss Velma Queen, Miss Ruth Abbey, Miss Florence Martin, and Miss Elizabeth Range—they loved and encouraged me to be my best, and I have very fond memories of them.

I recently completed an art piece; I call it *Snow Walk to School*. Only now do I see the absurdity of us Douglasville kids walking at least a mile to catch a school bus to ride another five miles to Douglass School. Rain or shine, snow and ice, we walked. Our destination was the steps of the all-white Central School, which we did not attend but which served as our bus stop. But integration finally put a stop to that.

THAT AMAZING DOUGLASS SCHOOL

The United States owes a great deal to Douglass School.

"There was no playbook," Larry Thompson said, recalling the attacks on September 11, 2001. Mere months before, he was sworn in as the deputy attorney general of the United States. "What happens when over three thousand of your fellow citizens are murdered? The mission of the Department of Justice changed overnight."

When the attacks occurred, Thompson was fifty-six years old. He was living in Washington and was quickly swept away by the Secret Service to a place so secure that even his wife didn't know where he was. Astonishingly, he was not the only Douglass alumnus to find himself in the high-profile position in the aftermath of the attacks.

Also in Washington that day was Brigadier General (Ret.) Donald L. Scott, who attended Douglass in the 1950s. He was CEO of the Library of Congress and had witnessed the plane hit the Pentagon, which was right across the Potomac River, as he was overseeing the evacuation of his employees. In Chicago, Joel Dant was the director of human resources for United Airlines, which lost sixteen employees in the attacks. He spent several days working around the clock to identify their remains and notify their families.

In the days, weeks, and months following the attacks, Thompson recalled, he found great purpose in his work, and he was guided by the values—hard, purposeful work without limitations—he traced back to his time growing up in Hannibal.

"Those seeds were planted at a little Colored school in northeastern Missouri," he said.

Thompson remembered Douglass School as small, modest, and supportive—a place embraced by all who attended. The teachers and administrators were from the community, many of them were Douglass and Lincoln University graduates, and they did the best with what limited resources were allotted to them by the city's segregated school district. Thompson vividly recalled that Douglass students were given hand-me-down books from the white school.

"I specifically remember my history teacher, Marion Powers. He was very outspoken about the fact that we had to work hard and that we had to be better than the other [white] person," Larry recalled.

Mr. Powers was also a community historian. Unfortunately for locals, both Black and white, the history of the Black community was nearly nonexistent in classrooms. We knew that some form of slavery existed. We knew that Blacks were treated very poorly. We knew that their life must have been degrading and impoverished, but records of this life had not been adequately researched until Mr. Powers. "Mr. Powers taught us Black history out of his hip pocket," Larry said of his old history teacher at Douglass. "I was taught about the East St. Louis and Tulsa race riots and abolitionist John Brown well before I entered junior high." They also had access to a 1930s-era Carter Woodson Negro history book.

The Douglass teachers were demanding with high expectations of their students. There were no excuses. Especially if you were bright—failure was unacceptable.

"The teachers were way more than educators," Brenda, Larry's sister, who was also a Douglass student, said. "They seemed to feel so much responsibility for the success of the Black community."

Growing up, the Thompsons knew that many Douglass graduates found success. Many went on to college at Lincoln University or another HBCU. Many became professionals and migrated to urban areas like St. Louis, Chicago, and Detroit.

Larry recalled the high expectations teachers at the school had for him. While he was a student at Douglass, he qualified for a countywide spelling bee. Many of his teachers came to watch as student after student dropped out of the competition. Eventually, it was just Larry and a white student from another Hannibal school.

Larry came in second place that day, stumbling over the spelling of a word he had practiced with his teachers at Douglass.

"One of them was very, very upset with me," Larry said, chuckling over the idea of being upset with a student who got second place. "She said, 'Young man, if you're going to be a success in life, you have to work harder.' There were no 'attaboys' that day."

Brenda had a similar memory of her fifth-grade teacher at Douglass: "Mrs. Weatherall. Most memorable for lots of reasons. She took spelling very seriously, and we got a lick with a ruler for each misspelled word. I still can't spell arithmetic. But she taught us so much more than the expected literature of Paul Lawrence Dunbar and Langston Hughes."

Larry entered the ninth grade at the brand-new junior high that was built to accommodate the influx of new Black students. His sister, Brenda, entered the sixth grade at Eugene Field School. "I hated that school, I always felt like an outsider," she said.

Douglass made Larry and Brenda's transition to their integrated public schools easier. They were more than prepared socially and academically, and above all, they were confident. But it was years before either Larry or Brenda encountered another Black teacher again, especially one that seemed to have such a vested interest in their success.

"I owe a great deal of gratitude to the really dedicated teachers at Douglass School," Larry said. "And those teachers, certainly, never—ever—taught us that there were limitations to what we could do if we were committed."

Brenda added: "I loved Douglass. That's where my friends, my neighbors, my mentors were." Teachers realized that integration meant an upgrade in resources for their students, though they also understood it meant they would

Teachers supervise Douglass students during recess. Despite our teachers' best efforts, because our schools received far less financial support from the racist Hannibal Public School District, the buildings were in a constant state of disrepair. For example, in 1922, Hannibal voters approved a bond issue of $600,000 for schools. $200,000 went to rebuild North School and rename it Pettibone School in honor of the donor. Another $100,000 went to Central School, $150,000 to Eugene Field, $125,000 to Stowell, and poor ole Douglass received just $23,000 to install indoor plumbing. We not only had fewer textbooks, but most were used and outdated hand-me-downs from Hannibal's white schools. The underpaid staff did what they could with little support, and for that we are grateful.

VELMA O. QUEEN
Grade One
A.B.
Howard University-Washington, D.C.

RUTH M. ABBEY
Grade Two
B.S.
Lincoln University-Jefferson City, Missouri

FLORENCE S. MARTIN
Grade Three and Four
B.S., M.S.
Kansas State Teachers College, Pittsburg, Kansas

THELMA H. FORTE
Grade Five
B.A.
Lincoln University, Jefferson City, Missouri

CAROLYN G. RANGE
Grade Six and Seven
A.B., M.A.
Lincoln University, Jefferson City, Missouri

MARY C. GRIFFIN
Grade Eight and Phy. Education
B.S.
Lincoln University, Jefferson City, Missouri

Here, nearly twenty years later, the last photograph of teachers from the 1955 yearbook. With the announcement that Douglass was going to close, the teachers included the importance of good hygiene in their lectures to students headed to the new white schools, right along with stressing about the importance of academic success. Douglass pride!

THOMAS W. MILLER
Industrial Arts & Math.
B.S.
Lincoln University, Jefferson City, Missouri

ELIZABETH R. RANGE
English
A.B.
Lincoln University, Jefferson City, Missouri

O. E. ESTILL
Science & Phy. Education
B.S., M.S.
Lincoln University, Iowa University

ELLA D. HOBBS
Home Economics
B.S.
Lincoln University, Jefferson City, Missouri

J. L. BROOKS
Music & Math.
A.B., M.A.
Lincoln University, Illinois University

MARION D. POWERS
Social Studies
B.S., M.A.
Lincoln University, Jefferson City, Missouri

A rare 1940s photograph of Douglass School teachers posing in front of the main building. Front row: Elizabeth Ross Range, Velma Queen, Grace Harmon, Edith Ross, Elizabeth Williams Range, Helen Carr, and Ella Bell Dant Hobbs. Back row: Oscar Estill, Inez Stevens, Edward January, Elva Clark, and Marion Powers.

likely lose their jobs. Sure enough, that fall, only three teachers received contracts: Miss Abby, Mrs. Carolyn Range, and Mr. Oscar Estill.

After he graduated Hannibal High School, Larry Thompson went on to Culver-Stockton College, Michigan State, and eventually law school at the University of Michigan. He became a successful attorney and was appointed by President George W. Bush in 2001 to be deputy attorney general of the United States. Retired, he now lives in Atlanta with his wife, Brenda. They have two sons. The couple are collectors of African American art, and they have amassed a remarkable collection of art from around the nation.

Brenda Thompson was educated in Missouri, graduating from Central Missouri State University. She is a retired elementary school teacher who taught in Rockford, Illinois, and Milwaukee, Wisconsin, for thirty years. She enjoys community history and traveling to African American historical sites.

Billy Morrison Jr. was born here in 1937. He is well-read and best described as a passionate historian. He has taken it upon himself to host monthly Black history classes at Willow Street Church, where an integrated group shows up. Those are his formal classes, but he also has a couple white fellas who show up at the local coffee shop for his lectures. Just like with his music, Billy is very informed and a joy to listen to.

Douglass School teachers Elizabeth Range (1902–2001) and Inez Stevens (1909–1982) spent their summer breaks traveling, photographed here at Pikes Peak, nearly eight hundred miles from home.

He's a professional jazz musician—very, very accomplished. When I asked who influenced him, he quickly responded: Mr. John L. Brooks (1908–1966). He taught music at Douglass. Mr. Brooks came here from Quincy and was a 1926 Douglass graduate. He received a BA from Lincoln and an MA from the University of Illinois. He was a World War II veteran, and he was only forty-seven years old when he lost his teaching job at Douglass. "He was a big influence on me," Billy said. "He took an interest in me on a personal level. He used to say, 'Billy, you can be anything you want to be.' In other words, he saw my potential."

Billy remembers the auditorium at Douglass—and is still outraged about one not-so-small detail. When the new space was built, everybody showed up to celebrate and watch the unveiling of the new curtain. Imagine the crowd's faces when a worn, red curtain was dropped. It was the old one from the white Hannibal High School; Douglass's school colors were blue and white.

Integration meant the immediate closure of the high school (grades ten, eleven, and twelve) and the letting go of many Black teachers. Many are surprised by how quickly we adapted as students and that there were few incidents. Joe Miller, who was in Hannibal's first integrated graduating class, recalls something different as more than one hundred white kids were kept home when school opened in September of 1955. "Fear of the unknown," he recalled.

The Douglass School marching band in the 1930s, a thirty-piece band that included students and some teachers. For years, the band was under the direction of Martin A. Lewis (1872–1945), who is remembered as the "Missouri Father of High School Bands." Mr. Lewis retired at seventy-two, after forty-four years of service as a DHS teacher and administrator.

Florence Martin (1897-1964), vacationing in Florida, lovely in her summer outfit and sweet smile. I don't recognize that sweet smile—she was very stern in class. She taught third grade until integration pushed her into retirement. Mrs. Martin was married to Rev. Earl Bryant Martin (1895-1962), pastor of an AME church in Kansas. She lived at 2116 Gordon Street.

Douglass lives on through the annual Douglass School reunion and scholarship events. The first reunion was in 1975 and the last was in 2015; many of the former students have passed on.

"DOUGLASS, DEAR OLD DOUGLASS, HOW I LOVE YOU..."

Mary Helen Holman Coleman can still remember what it was like being a little Black girl growing up under Jim Crow, running in and out of her mother's house at 2004 Spruce Street.

She called me recently. At the age of ninety-four, she has seen many things change in Hannibal, and she wanted me to know that in her day, kids didn't have any school cancellations for the weather; some of those kids walked nearly a mile to get to school, and others stood at bus stops in the harshest of weather.

Sitting in the home where she lives today—surrounded by beautiful landscapes, family photos, and her framed needlework—Mrs. Coleman shared her stories.

"We were just getting to be bold enough to speak up," she began. She remembered a day when, as a child, her older sister was at the butcher shop. The white clerk was ignoring her while waiting on white customers and spewing racial slurs. Finally, once he had

Mary Helen Holman Coleman's 1946 yearbook photo.

weighed, wrapped, and handed her the meat she ordered, she threw it at him and walked out of the store.

"I was so impressed with her courage," Mary Helen remembered. "And I hoped I would someday have that much courage. Well, sure enough, I was presented with a similar opportunity. One day I went to the Community Diary, and white teenagers came in after me. There was a white server behind the counter. After serving all the white kids, he asked me if I wanted 'vanilla like him or chocolate like me.' I told him, and after he handed me my cone, I smashed it down on the counter and sped out of the store."

Mary Helen's family has lived in Hannibal for generations. She was born in 1928—they were living at 426 Arch Street in the Bottoms, in a house and neighborhood she barely remembers. Both the house she was born in and the house she later moved to on Spruce are "empty lots now."

"My mother, Lucille Abbey Holman, had two sets of kids," she said. Mary Helen was one of nine. "She was in her forties when she had me, and called me a change-of-life baby. My oldest brother was twenty-six years older than me, and my oldest sister was twenty-four years older than me."

Henry Abbey—Lucille's father and Mary Helen's grandfather—was born in 1854 in Kentucky, enslaved. He was later brought to Perry, Missouri, before the family migrated to Hannibal, and he worked as a coach cleaner on the Burlington Railroad. Her grandmother, Lucille, did housework off and on.

"Yes, I grew up during segregation," Mary Helen said. "No signs, but we knew." That's why Douglass School tried to do so much with so little.

Mary Helen came of age at the height of Jim Crow and remembers well the crucial role Douglass played. In fact, she is one of the fortunate few still living who can actually remember even the layout of the school.

"We entered through the big front doors," she said. "Mr. Thurston was the janitor—you better not get caught running through those long hallways! Elementary school, and the principal's office, were on the first floor, with middle school and high school on the second. Every morning, the students started school by singing 'The Lord's Prayer,' accompanied on the piano by Miss Queen, a first-grade teacher who played beautifully. She used to say, we 'should be like a piano: grand, square, and upright!'"

Mary Helen and the other Douglass students learned way more than to read and write there. They learned culture and pride.

"We had operas, plays, talent shows, sports, scouts, clubs, PTA, chorus, and the best band in the state," she said with pride. "I remember one play performed only by our teachers. In fact, our music teacher, Miss Stephens, was from Hannibal and had an opera voice. Every spring we had an operetta. This was the only entertainment Black people had, and the auditorium would always be full of friends and relatives."

"I was a cheerleader," she said, smiling. "No, we didn't have uniforms. We once had a gymnastics program. It was led by Ms. Hayes, our new gym teacher—she had replaced Mr. Estill. Our mothers had sewed us matching outfits, and it was quite a hit!"

She went on: "Our home ec teacher, Mrs. Hobbs, and one of the senior girls, prepared all of our lunches. Sometimes

1954–1955 edition yearbook image of Coach Estill with members of his junior high basketball team. This team had the honor of winning the conference championship as well as the local Huck Finn Tournament. Opposing teams were from Dalton, Booneville, Columbia, Jefferson City, Monroe Holy Rosary, Christian Brothers Academy Monroe City, Sedalia, Shelbina, and Ilasco.

it was soup, or chicken, spaghetti, beans, and cornbread. Mainly the things we ate at home. Mrs. Hobbs, being a dietician, was a firm believer in healthy meals with fruits and vegetables." Mary Helen remembered Douglass as always being warm, comfortable, and very clean.

She continued: "After graduation, 1946, there were no jobs for us like the white girls got. Colored girls could only get jobs cooking or cleaning for white folks. My sister was a janitor at the Emporium Store and got me a job cleaning house for the mother of one of the clerks. I did my work, and at the end of the day, her mother told me to come to the back door next time. I went straight back to the daughter and told her I wouldn't be back if I had to come in the back. She had a talk with her mother, and I went back and entered through the front door. We had a second incident—this was about me using their bathroom, and again the daughter ran interference, saying her mother was old-school. I didn't work for this ole lady too long."

Mary Helen saw it all. She was thirty-six when the 1965 Civil Rights Act was passed, fifty-five when Hannibal elected Hiawatha Crow, its first—and only—Black member to the city council, and eighty when she helped vote in President Barack Obama.

"I just didn't see a reason to leave Hannibal," she says. "I married and raised four children here. I just wasn't the adventurous type."

Standing on her front porch, saying our goodbyes, Mary Helen pointed at a house on the other side of the street.

"My sister wanted to buy that house, but the owner would only sell it to a white family." Chuckling, she added that the "preferred owner's" daughter ended up with a Black man.

Sure enough, there are little Black grandkids running in and out of the house today.

Today, Mary Helen is a ninety-three-year-old Hannibalian surrounded by a loving family. She cares for her only living child, her son Craig, who lives with physical and mental challenges. She had three other children who are now deceased.

"Too bad we lost Mary Thurston Brown, she was the school historian—knew more than anybody about the history of the school," Mary Helen said. Mary lived on Arch Street, and a few years ago, she died there in a house fire, taking all the school records with her. Never-before-seen photographs and documents were lost. So much Douglass School history is gone forever.

Mr. Oscar Estill (1904–1982) was a graduate of Douglass School, Lincoln University, and Iowa State, where he earned his master's degree. He started his career at Douglass in 1957, where he taught PE, science, and math and coached track and basketball. Coach Estill shared that when he began his track-coaching career, he did not have a regulation track field to practice on but still produced a winning season every year. They ran the streets all around the school. He was hired at the new integrated junior high school in 1959, one of the three Colored teachers who got a job. He lived with his wife, Dorothy (1910–2008), and daughter, Gloria Sue, at 2308 Spruce Street and retired after forty-six years with the Hannibal Public School System.

DOUGLASS SCHOOL GRADUATES FROM 1878 TO 1955

1878
Braxton, Mary
Childs, Ida
Gibson, Eliza
Hubbard, Mary
Morris, Charles
Shortridge, Betty

1880
Brooks, Anna
Bruce, Luda
Hannox, Nellis
Hartman, Dora
Hartman, Mary
Howe, Eliza
Smith, Laura

1881
Damel, J. W.
Powers, William
Woodson, George

1887
Hopkins, Charles
Powers, George
Turner, Ella
1888
Taylor, Lulu Belle

1890-1891
Guy, Milton W.
Morris, Louis A.
Settles, Eliza
Roberts, William

1893
Fox, Jacob
Lewis, Martin
Randolph, James
Wallace, Albert

1896
Elgin, George
McGruder, William
Perkins, Mary

1899
Bolden, Cordelia
Bolden, Corinthia
Brock, Lucy
Foster, Ida M.
Hobbs, William
Lewis, Lulu
Phoenix. Edward
Robinson, Ada

1900
Braxton, Cora
Harris, Maude
Wright, William

1901
Gardner, Dottie
Hall, Della
Sexton, Alta

1902
Layson, Dora
Smith, Cameron
Spears, James
Taney, Bertha

1903
Phoenix, Laura Belle
Vivian, Jessie

1904
Kyles Nina
Morris, Nona
Sexton, Clara

1905
Lewis, Frank
McElroy, Amie
Robinson, Ella

1906
Ely, Martha
Helm, Ursie
Sanders, Mary
Sandidge, Bertha
Stevens, Mary

1907
Bell, Elnora
Bell, Matthew
Hopkins, Russell
Sanders, Emma
Sanders, Frances

1908
Hopkins, Katie
Laws, Mamie
Lewis, Lena
Randolph, Edith
Sexton, Beverly
Sandidge, Adah

1909
Berry, Matilda
Esque, Lizzie
Hueston, Elmer
Pelham, Alger

1910
Flood, Nellie
Fox. Alonzo
Fox, Alphonso
Lancaster, Lewis
McFadden, Emma Dell
Sanders, Katherine
Sanders, Mabel Lee
Stevens, James

1912
Howard, Sarah
Samuels, Sadie
Slayton, Vesper

1913
Allen, Onie
Howard, Isabelle
Randolph, Fannie
Robinson, Clara

1914
Monroe, Geneva
Simms, Emma

1915
Burton, Louise
Simms, Mary B.
Woods, Emily
Woodson, Mabel

1916
Abbey, Eliza
Powers, Latrelle
Roberts, Allene
Roberts, Rhoda
Wilson, Maceo

1917
Cotton, Sylvia
Sanders, Annie
Simms, Daisy
Simms, Ernest

1918
Britts, Clara
Cleaver, Arizona
Dant, Ella Belle
Parsons, Martha
Parsons, Mary
Russell, Ellie
Sexton, Joseph
Tucker, Jessie
Wright, Annie Mae

1919
Campbell, Harold
Drake, Melinda
Hughes, Willard
Powers, Lonesome
Randolph, Catherine

1920
Bell, Mabel
Douglas, Esque
Neal, Thelma

1921
Bell, Clara
Johnson, Lautenteen

1922
Coursey, Ethel
Jackson, Alice
Phillips. Elizabeth
Powers, Marion
Robinson, Wyneona
Ross, Cornelius

1923
Brown, Madeline
Coursey, Launie B.
Douglass, Walter
Estil, Oscar
Gibson, Wilfred
Laws, William
Longmire, Victor Hugh
Nickens, Elizabeth Anna

1924
England, Mary
Gardner, Candelaria
Gibson, Robert
Robinson, Reginald
Summerfield, Gertrude
Tapley, Evangelee

1925
Ashby, Helen
Batsell, Orville
Davis, Jericho
Mason, Hazel
Moore, Hiawatha
Robinson, Roscoe

1926
Anderson, Lela
Barber, Arlene
Brooks, John L.
Campbell, Loveliest
Carr, Helen
Douglass, Josephine
Gibson, Russell
Hawkins, William
Henderson, William

HANNIBAL'S INVISIBLES | 119

Johnson, Viola
Kyer, Emma
Mitchell, Mary
Robinson, George
Russell, Beatrice
Shannon, Louvester
Shropshire, Arthur

1927
Allen, Pearlie
Anderson, Everett
Ashby, Martha
Batsell, Elvena
Beatrice, Bell
Brown, Bertha
Green, Herbert
Harris, Dorsey
Jones, Rosalie
Kennedy, Ina
Lewis, Elizabeth
Marshall, William
Powers, Charles
Sephus, William
Stevens, Inez
Thurston, Helen

1928
Ambers, Thelma
Brown, Bernice
Coursey, Charles
Doolin, Maybe
Douglass, Ruth
Gibson, Edward
Hawkins, Laura Belle
Powers, Partea
Roberts, George
Brookside, Shannon
Whaley, Geraldine
Williams, Aurelius
Wilson, Carolyn
Wilson, Flossie

1929
Adams, Edgar
Hawkins, Romeo
Henderson, Kenneth
Holliday, Elsie
Howard, Rufus
Howard, Wilbur

Jewel, Vail
Kyer, Elmer
Longmire, Inez
Parson, Helen
Tate, Gilbert
Williams, Clarabelle

1930
Bell, Gerald
Bright, Clara
Combs, Gladys
Lewis, Mary Virginia
Morris, Lavetta
Perkins, Arnold
Riding, Albert
Robinson, Kermit
Ross, Beatrice
Steward, Frank
Wheeler, Charles

1931
Brooks, Gerald
Davis, Arnold
Grant, Shannon
Green, Arthur Ted
Harris, Wilbur
Holliday, William
Robinson, Doyo
Tate, Theodore
Wright, George Jr.

1932
Buckner, Neola
Claston, Flora
Douglass, Louise
Howard, Alonzo
Longmire, Bessie Lee
Robinson, Mattie H.
Rose, Julius Junus
Thurston, Mattie
Troy, Cecil
White, Genova
Wright, Hattie
Wright, Samuel

1933
Bright, Delbert
Crowe, Genevieve

Griffie, Maxwell
Hawkins, Dorothea
James, Wallace
Kelby, Helton
Lasley, Horatio
Lasley, Laura
Perkins, Owen
Thurston, Effie
Thurston, Mary
Welch, Cherish
Welch, Mildred

1934
Anderson, Myrtle
Ewing, Clay
Fox, Richard
Hobbs, Rebecca
Longmire, Vesper
McPike. Catherine
Nickens, Mildred
Thurston, James
Wesley, John
Williams, Gertrude
Williams, Marion
Williams, William

1936
Batsell, Emma
Black, James
Ely, Susie
Fike, Della
Hockett, Edna
Harrington, Iowa
Moore, Lucille
Morrison, William Frank
Williams, Louis
Wright, Booker
Wright, Isabelle

1937
Carter, Dorothea
Douglass, Helen
Ewing, Mildred Louise
Fox, Alonzo
Hopkins, Marjorie
Irving, Martha
Kyer, MaryAnne
Kyer, Ruth

Lewis, Lena
McPike, Orie
Moore, Thelma
Roberts, Mary Lee
Smith, Izetta
Turner, Edgell
Washington, Mary
Williams. Louise

1938
Brown, Elizabeth
Buckner. Lois
Caldwell, Emmitt
Harris, John T.
Harris, Isaac
Johnson, Clifford
Jones, Joseph
Longmire, Farrell
McAllister, Maude
Nearing, George
Powell, Gladys
Scott, Joseph
Simon. Reginald
Simpson, Lilllian
Williams, EulaMae

1939
Allen, Clyde
Allison, Sylvester
Ambers, Vincent
Anderson, Gertrude
Anderson, William
Banks, Cecil
Bell, Anita
Buckner, Oletha
Campbell, Mary
Cassidy, Lorraine
Cox, Edna Mae
Johnson, Ellen
Lasley. Isabelle
Lewis, Ida Mae
Morrison, Richard
Peters,, Dorothy Jane
Steward, Joseph
Steward, Geraldine
Tuck, Mary
Ward, Ida Mae

1940
Alexander, Suzanne
Bacquie, Genevieve
Brown, Phillip
Carter, Thomas
Cox, Mary E.
Green, George L.
Griggsby, Roberta
Houston, Juanita
Jackson, John
King, Ontario
Letcher, Robert
Madison, Amelia
McPike, Blair
Myers, Willa Frances
Nearing, Mary Lou
Reading, Ella
Riding, Vincent
Robinson, Frances
Robinson, Martha
Rose, Dorothy
Thurston, Aretha
Wright, DuBois

1941
Abbey, Humphrey
Alts, Helen
Anderson, Ada
Bell, Mary
Buckner, Frances
Campbell, Elizabeth
Cox, Hattie Belle
Felters, Opal
Harrington, Frances
Harris, John
Johnson, Betty
Lee, William
Mallory, Alene
Lewis, Kenneth
McElroy, Henry
Pelsue, Edna Iona
Reading, Florence
Shepherd, Ruth
Shepherd, Opal
Simpson, Helen
Stamps, Laura
Taylor, Alfretta
Turner, Ruth

Williams, Otis
Wright, Anna

1942
Bacquie, Leroy Francis
Bacquie. Rudolph Ernest
Brown, John Owen
Campbell, Keon
Cassidy, Donald Dumas
Clay, Mildred Helen
Daye, Flora Ruth
Johnson, Willa Mae
Lewis, Etta Mae
Miles, Margaret Florence
Myers, Dorothy Marie
Perkins, Sarah Louise
Richmond, Albert
Scott, Maude Pearl
Steward, Lucille Blane
Tate, Albert Walker
Williams, Harold
Williams, Lyle Ross

1943
Broadus, Quinault Vernell
Buckner, Margaret E.
Carter, Mabel D.
Demic, Sarah M.
Hall, Dumas Xanthanese
King, Marie L.
Kyer. Dora Louise
Lewis, Dorothy Marie
Longmire, Betty Mae
Paris, James Edward
Scott, Dorothy Mae
Webb, Ernest G.
Wesley, Maude E.
Williams, Libertad
Williams, Ruth M.

1944
Brown, Thelma Gertrude
Daye, Earl Jr.
Douglass, Betty Lou
Fountain, Myrtle Marie
Hale, Carl
Holman, Anna Gertrude
Johnson. Lucille B.
Thompson, Wanda
Woods, Dorothy Mae

1945
Buckner, Betty Jean
Buckner, William
Campbell, Betty
Cassady, Pvt. George W.
Cooper, Martha Ruth
Davis, Dorothy M.
Frazier, Mary Belle
Garr, Emma Elizabeth
Grant, Fred Oliver
Harding, Charles
Hughes, Mary
Johnson, Donald
Lewis, Mary Katherine
Mundy, Martha C.
Scott, Lillian V.
Williams, Kenneth

1946
Alexander, George
Bullock, Nathaniel
Campbell, Gertrude
Cassady, Kenneth
Fouche' Bonnie B.
Garr, Howard
Givens, Carolyn
Griggsby, Major Jr.
Harris. Carl
Holman, Mary Helen

Howard, Mildred
Longmire, Mary June
McElroy, Lillian
Smith, Darlene
Troy, Mary Frances
Williams, Joyce

1947
Abbey, Richard
Bacquie, Elaine
Campbell, Jerry
Clay, Ella
Dixon, Louise
Drake, Mildred
Frazier, Vincent Jr.
Gates, Christiana
Harding, Mary Lou
January, Julia
Johnson, Thomas
Kelly, Doolin
Kelley, Joanne
Mitchell, James Jr.
Morgan, Alva
Nearing, Frank
Smith, Clara
Smith, Robert
Smith, Van M.
Steward, Avis
Steward, Joyce
Steward, Loyce

1948
Allison, Inez
Crockett, Donald
Drake, Opal
Fountain, Albert
Gasberry, Thomas
Green, Rose Marie
Hall, Alonzo
Harrington, Alvin
Holliday, Ruth
Johnson, Imogen
Karr, Helen Marie
King, Katherine
Letcher, Hazel
Lewis, Norman
Marshall, James
Miller, Vyrle
Riding, Richard

Smith, James
Welch, Gale

1949
Abbey, Richard
Allen, Herbert
Britts, Harry
Buckner, George
Carter, Leonard
Crockett, Betty
Dudley, Ina Laura
Ford, Billy
Gray, Carl
Griggsby, William
Haley, Betty Jean
Howard, Sarah
Kerr, Russell
King, James
King, Velma
Madison. Majorie
Miller, Mary
Powell, Mary D.
Range, Kenneth
Steward, Ida Mae
Stamps, Henry
Turner, Mary
Williams, Emmitt

1950
Alls, Joanne
Bacquie. Marceline
Black, Clifton
Buckner. Hobert
Campbell, Etta Mae
Demic, James
Ford, Laura
Frazier, John
Gibson, Byron
Haley, Grace Ann
Hamilton, Shirley
Hawkins, Robert
Howard, Virginia Mae
January, Edward Jr.
Kelley, Archie
Mallory, Lloyd
McElroy, Glenside
Mcquay, Robert
Miles, Opal
Perkins, Fanny

Pleasant, Onella
Riding, Margaret
Woods, Barbara
Smith. Richard

1951
Allison. Arthaniel
Bryant, Nathaniel
Davis, Edward Linwood
Florence, Kenneth Leon
Gibson, Virginia Lotus
Grey, Betty
Hale, Vernier
Harrington, Leo
Linear, Howard
Majors, Maxie
McElroy, Hellmuth, Jr
Moore, James W.
Range, Joseph
Riding, James Orlando
Sephus, Marjorie
Snively, Patricia
Smith, Mary Ann
Stamps, Bertha E.
Steward, Emily
Tate, Harold Leon
Williams, Albert Jr.
Williams, Nadie

1952
Allen, Charlotte
Crockett, David Leon
Demic, Mary
Fisher, Hartwell
Garr, Billie June
Garr, Mary Lou
Gaskin, Bettie H.
Griggsby, Juanita
Holder, John
Kerr, Floyd Lee
McGruder, Richard
Miller. Austin
Miller, Barbara Jean
Miller, Jesse

Robinson, Jacqueline Faye
Robinson, Julia Luana
Sephus, Ann Marie #1
Smith. Kathleen Joyce #2
Woods, Harry Jr.
Woods, Joyce

1953
Biggs, Mary
Black. Raymond
Bridges, Ella
Bryant, James
Carter, Frances
Carter, Jeanne
Florence, Norman
Fox, Betty Lou
Green, Louise
Griggsby, Leona
Hall, Louis
Hickman, Ella
Harrelson, Guy
Jackson, Lloyd
Johnson, Mildred
Pinkard, Georgia Mae
Powers, Marion Jr.
Smith, Myrl
Snively, Lois
Steward, Odessa
Wallace, Laverne
Williams, James

1954
Cole, William Maurice
Fox, Alberta Belle
Gibson, Robert
Hale, Victor
Johnson, William
McElroy Gerald Jr. #2
McPike, Mary Elizabeth
Mahr, Wayne
Miles, Herman
Miller, Donald
Moore, Ernest
Moore, Joyce
Porter, David
Powers, Frances
Smith, Phillip #1
Stanton, Jerry
Weathers, Donald
Williams, Kenneth
Williams, Barbara

1955
Douglass, Shirley Ann
Frazier, Joe Louis
Lashley, Blondell
McBride, Lois William
McElroy, Mary Lucille #1
Porter, Charles
Wallace, Cristola
Ward, Velma Delores #2
Williams, James
Williams, Mona Lappacci
Woods, Choalotte Luella

Chapter 6

LET GO AND LET GOD

Nineteenth-century Missouri law forbade the "unsupervised" (meaning white-supervised) assembly of Black people in large groups for any purpose, including worship. Despite the existence of such laws, and despite frequent threats and lack of finances, local Blacks founded the first church in 1853, the African Church. Here, they gathered to worship and defined freedom of religion for themselves. While the earliest church was founded by free Blacks, most of its members were enslaved. Churches also played an important role in Black life, providing a key source of social contact and relief. Collectively, churches represent the oldest institution created and controlled by African Americans. From its beginning during slavery, the Black church has stood as the foundation of worship and of political, economic, and social life. In Hannibal's early days, all denominations shared one building for worship services until other churches were built some years later.

EIGHTH AND CENTER STREETS MISSIONARY BAPTIST CHURCH

Eighth and Center Streets Missionary Baptist Church is one of two churches in the Maple Avenue Historic District. A long way from its original log cabin, it's a Romanesque Revival constructed from Missouri redbrick. Its two-story rectangular building faces Center Street. In 1903, a brick parsonage was built directly adjacent to the back of the church facing Eighth Street, at 204 N. Eighth Street. Located in the basement is the baptismal, the kitchen, the dining room, and Sunday School classrooms. The upper level features the sanctuary, the choir stand, and the pastor's office and living quarters.

This very impressive structure is one of the most notable buildings in Hannibal and a principal historical landmark of the African American community. The cupolas visible no longer exist.

The current building is the second church erected on these grounds. Members and visitors enter through a beautiful round-arched doorway with two red wooden doors that were installed in 1959. After entering, you will encounter a dual set of stairs, each walking up twenty steps to enter the sanctuary—a very rickety and somewhat dangerous journey for all who enter.

We have two church historians to thank for documenting its history: lifelong members Edward January and Hiawatha Crow. From them we learn that Hannibal's oldest surviving Black church began with the 1853 split with white Baptists, which was not a pretty split. The land on which the church now stands was purchased for $37.50 on April 22, 1853, by free persons of color. The first and most important leader was O. H. Webb, who pastored here for forty years; he is the longest-serving pastor in Hannibal's history. From 1901 to 1916, Rev. C. R. McDowell provided amazing leadership, adding the parsonage, cupolas, stained glass windows, and sidewalks. These stained glass windows were donated by various community leaders and fraternal organizations. Since then, there have been a number of preservation efforts and visits by a number of prestigious early Baptist church leaders. The site's rich history cannot be denied.

Patricia Blackwell Snoddy grew up attending the Eighth and Center Streets Missionary Baptist Church, and it shaped her life in ways she never could imagine. For better or worse, church is like family.

"As far back as I can remember, my adopted mom, Pauline Blackwell (1910–2009) is sitting bone straight, Bible in hand, third row back on the left, facing the pulpit," Pat

A photograph from the 1963 church anniversary program showing the Junior Choir with Director Elsie Gibson Perkins and the pianist, Nora Frances Demic. Patricia Blackwell, a member since infancy, is the tallest girl in the photograph.

remembered. "She's behind Mrs. Roberts, church secretary, seated next to a beautiful stained glass window. As I grew up, the ministers changed every few years, but the congregation remained the same."

She added with a laugh: "They didn't even change seats!"

"I've been coming here since I was a baby," Pat said. "My adopted mother, Pauline, was a lifetime member. My foster father, Theodore Blackwell, went to Allen Chapel AME Church. As a fourteen-month-old infant, I likely ate and slept during those three hours of church, which began with Sunday school at 10:00 a.m. every Sunday morning of my life."

"Me, in my cute little starched dress," she continued. "At about four, I started going to Sunday school, it was in the basement. This is where I met my first best friends, even before Douglass School. It was me, Shelia, Rhoda, VanDel, and Abraham. Elsie or Dottie, my Sunday school teachers, always smelling like peppermint from partying the night before!"

Pat recalled how the church filled so much of her time. There was choir rehearsal, Wednesday Bible study, Girls Action Missionary Club—the "GA"—the Sunshine Club, revivals, and Vacation Bible School. As she described it, church was "way more than Sunday morning. We usually went back Sunday evening, unless there was an event at another church. Those churches were all in the countryside, most not as big or fancy as ours, but the choirs were as good, and the food was better."

She continued, "We had our own kitchen committee and the best cooks in town who were responsible for all meals for baptisms, funeral repasts, pastor anniversaries, Choir Day, Christmas, Easter, and visits from other churches. Menus didn't change. There was always ham, fried chicken, baked chicken and dressing, homemade rolls, vegetables, and salads and desserts galore."

As she recalled, "All these church ladies were mostly widows. Women always outlived the men."

Pat was fifteen when she had her first daughter, Renee. This changed everything with her adopted mother. It was also about this same time when she met her biological mother and her ten siblings. To her surprise, they had been her neighbors, schoolmates, and friends all her life—unbeknownst to her.

"Imagine playmates who were actually my siblings," Pat said, and a mother and sister and brothers who loved her and accepted "the willful child" like her adopted mother never did. About the same time, Pat learned that it was these same Eighth and Center church ladies who had convinced the authorities that her birth mother, "Mother Ruby," was unfit, and so they adopted out all her children.

"I realize now that 'Mother Pauline' sometimes mistreated me because she knew I'd never love her like my real family," Pat lamented.

Patricia Blackwell Snoddy is an amazing woman who has overcome many challenges thrown at her. She is not quite retired, quite striking, and very fit, and she volunteers with a local food bank where she feeds and counsels some of Hannibal's most down-and-out residents. She regularly gives blood to the Red Cross. She is the mother of four children and six grandchildren. She recently lost her son, Taurean Snoddy (1984–2023), in a violent crime that is still being investigated.

A PARTIAL LIST OF HANNIBAL'S EARLY BLACK CHURCHES

Second Christian Church

Their minister, Rev. Raymond Brown, initiated the purchase of the old Douglass School building for the new home of Second Christian Church in 1960. It was a memorable day as members gathered at the former Broadway church and took that ceremonial walk to the new church at 404 Willow Street. Members soon rechristened it Willow Street Christian Church, and "second to no one was the consensus."

Second Christian reclaims Douglass School. This photo shows the congregation's move from Broadway to Willow.

A 1933 photograph of the Second Christian Church at 1614–1618 Broadway. The original church on this site was built in 1874 and torn down in 1917, and this stone church building was built. This church building was razed in 1965, and the site returned to its original appearance—woods and overgrown weeds.

Rev. Isaac Haley and congregation. Marsha Mayfield, a community historian and youth leader, recognizes some faces: "I see Rev. Haley (seated with the blank sign). Sister Haley is standing in the third row behind him next to the woman in white. Next to her is Haley's uncle. Rev. Johnson, he is wearing the striped tie. Best guess is a few of his children are also in the photograph. He had nine.

There were a number of transitions before the original school was demolished. For a number of years, the former school housed several community services programs that filled a void for the most vulnerable and became the foundation for our existing Douglass Community Services. Willow Street's Reverend Meeker led the effort.

Hannibal's Church of God and Christ

Hannibal's Church of God in Christ, Inc. (COGIC) is a Christian organization in the Holiness-Pentecostal tradition. Predominantly African American, it is the largest Pentecostal denomination in the United States. It was founded in 1907 by Bishop Charles H. Mason, a son of a former slave. It was Elder W. L. Johnson who was responsible for erecting the Pentecostal Church at 912 Settles Street in 1929. Residents who lived near this Settles Street Holy Church share memories of a booming choir and popular catfish dinner fundraisers.

The most recent owner of the little Settles Street structure was the Fannie Griffin Arts Club, an organization dedicated to uplifting Hannibal's African American women and children. The building had been long abandoned when it was razed by the city in 2018. The cornerstone was donated to Jim's Journey and can be seen on the museum grounds.

Allen Chapel AME Church

It won't surprise you to learn that many of the original members of this and all of Hannibal's early churches were formerly enslaved, or just one generation removed. This included Lena Doolin Mason (1864–1924). Mason was the daughter of Von Puhl (Vaughn) and Cerilda Doolin, a local couple who escaped slavery when Von Puhl ran away from his Missouri enslaver to join the Union army in Quincy, Illinois. After the war, the newly emancipated

Another one of the city's earliest Black churches, Allen Chapel AME Church was organized in 1869. This structure was built at 806 Church Street in 1930. The federal building, post office, and parking lot now stand where the original church stood. This vulnerable old church was moved from this site in 1966 to an area known as Williamsville; the new property was purchased for the church at 101 S. Hawkins. The church has struggled for several years to maintain a congregation.

family returned to Hannibal and lived in Douglasville. Because of her father's courage, Lena was born a free woman. She was also a Douglass School student, and a wife, mother, evangelist, and a poet.

At twenty-three, Lena entered the ministry and became a successful and widely recognized traveling evangelist. Lena is also one of our earliest, but lesser-known, African American poets. One of her pieces, "A Negro in It," pays homage to "Big Jim Parker," the Black man who bravely attempted to stop Leon Czolgosz from assassinating President McKinley in 1901:

A Negro in It
Lena Doolin Mason

In the last civil war,
The white folks, they began it,
But before it could close,
The Negro had to be in it.

At the battle of San Juan Hill,
The rough-riders they began it;
But before victory could be won
The Negro had to be in it.

The Negro shot the Spaniard from the tree,
And never did regret it;
The rough-riders would have been dead to-day
Had the Negro not been in it.

To Buffalo, McKinley went,
To welcome people in it;
The prayer was prayed, the speech made,
The Negro, he was in it.

September sixth, in Music Hall,
With thousands, thousands in it,
McKinley fell, from the assassin's ball,
And the Negro, he got in it.

He knocked the murderer to the floor,
He struck his nose, the blood did flow;
He held him fast, all nearby saw,
When for the right, the Negro in it.

J. B. Parker is his name,
He from the state of Georgia came;
He worked in Buffalo, for his bread,
And there he saw McKinley dead.

They bought his clothes for souvenirs,
And may they ever tell it,
That when the President was shot
A brave Negro was in it.

He saved him from the third ball,
That would have taken life with it;
He held the foreigner fast and tight,
The Negro sure was in it.

McKinley now in heaven rests,
Where he will ne'er regret it;
And well he knows, hat in all his joys
There was a Negro in it.

White man, stop lynching and burning
This black race, trying to thin it,
For if you go to heaven or hell
You will find some Negroes in it.

Parker knocked the assassin down,
And to beat him, he began it;
In order to save the President's life,
Yes, the Negro truly was in it.

You may try to shut the Negro out,
The courts, they have begun it;
But when we meet at the judgment bar
God will tell you the Negro is in it.

Pay them to swear a lie in court,
Both whites and blacks will do it;
Truth will shine, to the end of time,
And you will find the Negro in it...

from Negro Poets and their Poems, *published by Robert Kirlin in 1923.*

Rev. Lena Doolin Mason, a notable AME evangelist. Lena married George Mason (1848–1929), with whom she had six children. Credit: Minnesota Historical Society.

In this early 1900s photo, children pose in front of Scott's Chapel. Scott's Chapel will soon celebrate 150 years as a congregation and one hundred years in their current building at 1815 Hope Street.

Scott's Chapel United Methodist Church

Lola Richardson's church history reads: "Scott's Chapel was organized in 1887 in Brittanham Hall on Broadway, two years after the first two Black congregations were organized. They were Allen Chapel, AME, and Eighth and Center Street Missionary Baptist churches. Scott Chapel was named after the first 'Negro missionary' Bishop Isaiah B. Scott. The first pastor and organizer Rev. Jeremiah Wright."

The current stone church resembles a castle, since the congregation bought the building in 1917. It's known as the church on the corner with a big heart; a beacon in a somewhat depressed area challenged by poverty, addiction, and violent crime. The stone church on the corner includes a mission to "be there" through hard times. The community all come out to celebrate an annual block party—clean family fun.

Helping Hand Baptist Church

A dedicated congregation worshiped in its small brick sanctuary for many years, organized after a split with Eighth and Center Streets Missionary Baptist Church in 1916. When Kevin Bruce Taylor was growing up, he and his family were members there. He talked about those long church Sundays when his parents would get him and his brother, CV, up early and into their "church clothes." Taylor recalled them being two of the best-dressed boys in church: "My mom was an excellent seamstress and made a lot of our clothes. First, we attended Sunday School where kids were organized by age and reading ability to spend the morning learning Bible stories. Then for 11:00 a.m. services, we'd head to where the adults were, that was another two hours. And unless there was an event being sponsored by another local church, we headed back to Helping Hand for another service in the evening."

Helping Hand Baptist Church, 1020 Lyon Street, small brick building built in 1917 under the leadership of Rev. C. R. McDowell. This humble little structure was recently replaced with a beautiful new building adjacent to this.

He said, "I recall a lot of hootin' and hollerin' and people speaking in tongues, just had to let loose. There was the piano player and an awesome choir, and some of them could really thump! My father, Charles Taylor, was one of them; he even joined a men's choir, the Mighty Men of Song. Back then, when there was a death in the congregation, the church was responsible for the funeral service and the repast; it seems like everybody in town showed up for a funeral. There were some great cooks, I'll tell you. I remember them ladies would be in the kitchen, cooking up a storm."

Like the Taylors, it seemed like most families in Hannibal had a similar relationship with church: it was a daylong commitment. Outside the pulpit, like Dr. King, Rev. Jones can be described as a force for equal rights in the community. "He opened a lot of doors for some good paying jobs for Black people in Hannibal," Taylor said, and he recalled that Rev. Jones even became president of the NAACP. "While I don't know for sure," he said, "it wouldn't surprise me to learn that Rev. Jones was in the crowd when we drove George Wallace out of town."

And like most Black communities across the United States, church was—and is—an important institution in Hannibal, particularly during the civil rights movement, which many ministers and church leaders from all denominations had an integral role in.

"This was every Sunday. It was what we did. It was always good to fellowship with friends and family, I will never forget it." Taylor also recalled one important pastor from that period: "His name was Rev. Jewell Jones. As a kid, I was probably most fascinated with the fact that he only had one leg; it had been amputated when he was young, wish I knew what really happened. But boy, he'd get in that pulpit—and I mean to tell you, he'd strut up and down, waving that Bible in his hand, preaching the Word. He lit up our little church."

Chapter 7

ALL GAVE SOME, SOME GAVE ALL

African Americans have fought, and many have died in every US conflict. In my white high school, I learned about Crispus Attucks, a Black man who was struck down during the American Revolution, but it wasn't until I got to college that I learned the contributions of enslaved and free Blacks who contributed so much to win the Civil War. At the integrated Hannibal High School, we were taught that Black people were "lounging on the beach," waiting for the war to end—wrong.

More than 180,000 Black men, women, and children performed many functions in the war. In 1864, Union generals opened a recruiting office here in Hannibal, where runaway slaves gathered to enlist. There were seven African American regiments enlisted in the Union—one African American unit in Missouri included a state militia from Hannibal and had nearly one hundred members. These soldiers fought in battles in Tennessee, Louisiana, Texas, and Alabama. I can only imagine the pride our veterans would feel when they discovered their name on the list of US Civil War Draft Registrations Records—even more pride in being identified as a runaway while their enslavers put on gray uniforms and sought reimbursement for their lost "property." Runaways came from Marion, Pike, and Ralls Counties. Black carpenters, cooks, guards, laborers, nurses, scouts, spies, and steamboat pilots—many died before, during, and soon after the war.

More than two dozen local United States Colored Troops Civil War veterans' tombstones have been identified at the Old Baptist Cemetery. William Morrison is one of several local USCT gravesites that have been identified. Morrison returned home after the war and lived out his life here. Mr. Morrison married Jeanetta Givens Morrison (1849–1932), and they had three children: Arthur, George, and Arzola. William is last found on

the 1900 Census. From all indications, he could read and had one formerly enslaved neighbor on his street—Louella Tate, born in 1862, was found washing and ironing for a living. His descendants still live in Hannibal today.

Even in the face of segregation and racism, Hannibal's Black community joined other Americans doing their part fighting for, and with, the United States in every conflict. Despite the discrimination—less pay, inferior weapons and materials, and inadequate medical care—that followed them into the military, and then home when their service ended.

When Americans were enlisting for World War I, Clarence Woodson was only twenty-one years old when he joined the fight. He lived at 2511 Hope Street and worked at the Hannibal Wheel Factory. His parents, James Sr. and Emily Woodson, were formerly enslaved. Private Woodson served in the 366th Infantry Regiment, 92nd Division during the war. He was killed on November 11, 1918, the very day the armistice ending the war was signed. He is buried in St. Mihiel American Cemetery in Thiaucourt, France. His older brother, James Woodson (1891–1961), fought in World War II. Fortunately, he returned to Hannibal, married, and died here at home in 1961.

Rev. C. R. McDowell, minister of Helping Hands Baptist, collaborated with Scott's Chapel Church to give our men a proper send-off. I learned that they organized a parade to honor the twelve recruits headed to war in 1918. The parade included the recruits, the school band, the Negro Red Cross volunteers, fraternal organizations, and flag-waving schoolchildren.

When these early Black Hannibalians who fought and served were left out of local veterans' service organizations, they started their own. On September 6, 1919, the Negro veterans came together to organize the Colored American Legion Post #155. Twenty-four

Clarence Woodson (1897–1918), a World War I veteran. He was born in Hannibal.

Right: World War I veteran Gerald McElroy Sr. (1902–1979) in full military uniform.

Veteran Of Two World Wars Dies; Funeral Saturday

Thomas J. Marcellus, 67, of 504 Lemon St., was pronounced dead upon arrival at St. Elizabeth Hospital Tuesday morning at 10:15. He was a veteran of both World War I and World War II.

Services will be conducted at 2 o'clock Saturday afternoon at the Robinson Mortuary. Rev. Raymond E. Brown, pastor of Second Christian Church will officiate and interment will be in the Robinson Cemetery.

Friends may call at the mortuary after 5 o'clock Thursday evening.

Military rites will be conducted Friday night at 7:30 at the mortuary by the Clarence Woodson Post No. 155, American Legion.

Mr. Marcellus was a member of the Allen Chapel AME Church.

He is survived by an uncle, James G. Marcellus and a niece, Mrs. Louis (Clara Belle) Bright, both of Hannibal and four nephews, Humphrey Abbey of Indianapolis and Richard, Melvin and Howard Owen Abbey, all of Maywood.

Died Nov-30th 1965

Left: The heroics of Thomas Marcellus (1898–1965), a local with the distinction of serving in both World War I and World War II, are also interesting. He was living on Lemon Street when he died at age sixty-seven. I'd say he lived a full life. His niece, Clarabelle Bright, was the only local relative to attend the service.

Herbert Britts (1904–1965), World War II veteran. Herbert was married to Grace Grant Britts (1911–1952). This photograph was donated by a very proud granddaughter, Patricia Holman.

PFC James C. Brown, born in 1930, served with the 24th Division in Korea when he was reported missing in action. James had lost his mother, Susie Brown (1890–1937), at seven years old. His father, Frank Matthew Brown (1888–1958), was a World War I veteran who died shortly after James was reported missing. The fact that James never came home likely tugged at his father's heart until his dying day.

Reported Missing

PFC James C. Brown (above), serving with the 24th division in Korea, has been reported missing in action. His father, Frank Matthew Brown, lives at 418 North Ninth street.

Two brothers: Kenneth Williams (1926–1989, left) and Lyle Ross Williams (1922–1997, right). Both served in the Buffalo Division of the Armed Forces. The 92nd Infantry Division (Buffalo) was the only African American infantry division to see combat in Europe during World War II, fighting in the Italian campaign. African Americans in all other units were used as support personnel—menial labor.

Top: Estel Griggsby (1912–2017), a navy man based in Pearl Harbor, Hawai'i.

Left: His brother William (who is still living in Washington, DC).

Top: Estel's brother James (1920–2011).

Right: Estel's brother Major (1928–2020).

A gathering of veterans. Left to right: Leland Perkins, Estel Griggsby, Albert Fountain, Louis Bright, Walter Sutton, Ora Hart, and Maceo Wilson.

Left: Sgt. James Alfred Smith (1926–1979). The 1955 census lists that he and his wife, Hazel, lived on Minnow Street. "Dad was a body man at Murphy Motors and also had his own garage," recalled James's daughter, Candy Smith Weems. She grew up with this photograph of her dad sitting on top of the TV in their Gordon Street living room. Candy, born in 1957, is a community volunteer and the dedicated caretaker of her ninety-plus-year-old mother who still lives on Gordon Street, the street she grew up on. And like her father, Candy has been a hard worker all her life.

members enrolled at that first meeting that was held at Douglass School. Another World War I veteran, Maceo Wilson, led the effort. By his side was Olie Slayton and Willard B. Hughes. It was decided that it would be named for Clarence Woodson, who died in Europe the day the armistice to end World War I was signed. He was among the last victims of the war.

For many years, the Clarence Woodson Post #155 met at 1220 Girard Street. It was a place where friends and families of Black veterans could gather with dignity and receive community recognition for their service. The place would not have functioned without the ladies' auxiliary, who fed patrons and sponsored dances and fundraisers.

A NEW HOME FOR POST #155

2205 Market became the new home of the Colored American Legion Post #155. Sadly, they got into financial trouble soon after they acquired the property.

When Sonny Fitzpatrick, veteran and a businessman, heard that the legion was up for auction because of back taxes, he knew he had to do something. "It was the last standing symbol dedicated to those who faithfully and honorably served our country," he said, "a place where Black folks could gather for a drink, a bite to eat, and some R&B music had to be rescued."

He purchased the building but determined it was best if he reopened it as Fitz's Lounge. Blacks had a place of their own for another twenty-five years.

With this change, Sonny convinced local veterans to donate several items to Jim's Journey to ensure the story of Post #155 continued. On display for all to see is the sixty-inch Colored American Legion Post #155 banner, a thirty-six-by-forty-inch image of uniformed Clarence Woodson, and the Stag Beer chandelier that hung over the pool table at the Girard Street location for many years.

Post #155 reopened at 2205 Market Street. Veteran Albert Fountain (1929-2004) was put in charge of running things. A veteran committed to his duties as a member of the Clarence Woodson American Legion Post #155, he was commander of the post and sergeant of the honor guard. He recruited his wife, Mary Lucy Dorsey (1934-2004), to help; she had been a member of the ladies' auxiliary. When you saw Albert, you saw Lucy—they were inseparable. Mr. Fountain, from Mexico, Missouri, was a US Army veteran of the Korean War. He was a Mark Twain Hotel employee when he enlisted at only eighteen years old. After military service, he was a truck driver for Schwerman Trucking Co., and when he retired, he became a custodian for Hannibal Public Schools. In later years, when the two American Legions closed, Mr. Fountain transferred his allegiance to Post #55.

Miss Mary L. Roberts, above, daughter of Mr. and Mrs. George E. Roberts, 1104 North street who was enrolled in the Women's Army Auxiliary Corps January 8, is awaiting call for active service. Miss Roberts graduated from Douglass High school in 1937, attended Lincoln University for two years and received her B. S. degree in home economics in 1942 from West Virginia State College. She is a member of Delta Sigma Theta sorority and Home Economics Club.

This photograph appeared in Hannibal's local newspaper, the *Courier-Post*. Mary L. Roberts Williams (1921–2002) was visiting her family in Hannibal when it was taken.

Hannibal Woman Helping Celebrate WAC Anniversary

SP5 ADAH ANDERSON

SP5 Adah E. Anderson, daughter of Mrs. Samuel H. Smith, 715 Hill Street, is celebrating the Women's Army Corps 20th Anniversary. She was sworn in the Corps on February 11, 1943 and went on active duty, April 4 of the same year. She began her 18½ years service at Fort Des Moines, Iowa, where she took basic training.

Photo of retiring Adah Anderson McPike (1920–1992). She was the daughter of Barbara Smith and was a Douglass School graduate who enlisted in the WAC in 1943. She retired after twenty years of service and world travel.

SKIRTED SOLDIERS—CWO US ARMY

Mary L. Roberts Williams was the daughter of local undertaker George Roberts (1883–1967) and his wife, Bertha (1884–1978). Her brother, George "Brooksey" Roberts, preceded her in death. She enrolled in the Women's Army Auxiliary Corps (WAAC), and in September 1943, Congress authorized the Women's Army Corps (WAC), which made women regular army. The first women arrived at the first WAAC Training Center at Fort Des Moines on July 20, 1943. Among them were 125 enlisted women and 440 officer candidates (forty of whom were Black), who had been selected to attend the WAAC Officer Candidate School, or OCS. The WACs served in all three areas of the army: the Army Air Forces, the Army Service Forces, and the Army Ground Forces. Mary graduated from Douglass School in 1937 before attending Lincoln University and West Virginia State College. She married John Williams, lived in St. Louis, and was buried at Jefferson Barracks National Cemetery in St. Louis when she died.

VIETNAM

Larry Oliver Green in Vietnam. He joined the Army in 1972, served two tours in Vietnam, and retired after a twenty-year career. He's quick to say that he didn't like Hannibal, describing it as a racist, hostile little town, one not very nice to him. He remembers struggles with school integration, getting slapped in the face by his fourth-grade teacher, and racial discrimination on the high school basketball court. He left to join the military at seventeen and never looked back. Never would have realized his full potential here.

NEVER EASY

From the start, Black veterans had trouble dealing with racism in the military. That was never more true or devastating than for World War II veterans. Roosevelt signed the Servicemen's Readjustment Act into law on June 22, 1944, only weeks after the war ended. It ushered into law sweeping benefits for veterans, including college tuition, low-cost home loans, and unemployment insurance. Racism was blatant and impactful for our returning 1.2 million Black World War II vets. Securing the GI Bill's benefits promised to all became hampered when the federal government turned over its administration to the states. While the racist denial of benefits may have been more flagrant in the South, the North was just as guilty.

What history deniers don't want you to learn is that while the Readjustment Act helped white Americans prosper and accumulate wealth in the postwar years, it didn't deliver on that promise for veterans of color. The truth about the wide disparity gaps in wealth, education, and civil rights between white and Black Americans is what many want kept out of history books.

In 1949, the nineteen-year-old Robert Mattox (1924–2002), with full knowledge of the GI Bill, applied to Hannibal Public Schools' Vocational Training School for automotive repair training. He was rejected—"NO NEGROES ALLOWED"—despite the education benefit promising educational training to all soldiers. It wasn't until after the local schools integrated in 1955 that these vets were admitted: Kenneth Henderson, Robert Mattox, Kenneth Williams, and Wallace Dixon.

Chapter 8

ORGANIZING FOR CHANGE

Despite numerous laws ending legalized discrimination, Black people continue to struggle against racism, segregation, inequality, and injustice. Early on, we began banding together in fraternal organizations, political organizations, and clubs. This was supported by individual attempts to run for local offices, hoping for a seat at the table—thought to be one of the most powerful tools to improve the economic, educational, employment, and general living conditions for Black people. Fortunately, the National Association for the Advancement of Colored People has deep roots in Hannibal.

But it wasn't just our leaders who stood up. In ways small and large—visible and invisible—Black Hannibalians challenged the system. Ruth Hunter Linear, for example, was one of the first Black students to integrate Hannibal High School. Ruth was a classmate and a friend to my aunties G. G., Edna, and Mayna. She spent a lot of time at my grandmother's house at 202 Olive Street. I once had the opportunity to ask about her integration experience—"What was it really like those first weeks?"—and she told her story with a mischievous grin (she is an awesome storyteller):

> I believe it was gym class, we had to partner up, for a game. A to-remain-anonymous white girl made it clear that she wasn't going to be my partner, she even said, "We don't want to go to school with you Niggers, no way." I told the teacher, but the white girl lied and said she didn't say it. The teacher pretended to believe her and disregarded my complaint. But I paid her back. I knew the girl. Me and my mom did her laundry. Not long after the incident, I showed up at school wearing her clothes—nice skirts

and blouses. I did this for several weeks. She didn't dare say anything. Here I was, wearing her expensive clothes from Kleins, Emporium, and the Famous [upscale women's clothiers]. I figured if I had to wash and iron her skirts and blouses, I would just wear them. Especially since she had called me out of my name and didn't get in any trouble. And that's what I did. My outfits would include fancy skirts, blouses, all topped off with her neckerchief. I went to school sharp! Every time the girl got new clothes, it meant that I did, too. Mama eventually lost the job because of me, I got a whipping. Mama was a parent who didn't play when it came to discipline. But the whipping was worth it.

FRATERNAL ORGANIZATIONS AND CLUBS

Hannibal in the late 1800s was best described as energetic and expanding. The same can be said of the recently emancipated Black community in town. Segregated fraternal organizations had a role in this growth. Our 1927 Colored Directory lists five Prince Hall Mason lodges, two Odd Fellow lodges, four temples of United Brothers of Friendly (UBF), and eleven temples for women's organizations, including the Masonic Eastern Stars. They cared for orphans, widows, the poor, and the aged; they were a moneylender, a place where one could get a job reference, secure school supplies, church donations, and more. They were family oriented, and full of fun and games.

These organizations provided a unified response to racism and promoted the values of honesty and hard work. Members of these lodges included the ordinary and the extraordinary. They were made up of some of the most prominent members of our community: veterans, physicians, nurses, policemen, morticians, ministers,

A rare photograph of unidentified local Masons from 1904. One of Hannibal's first chapters of Black Prince Hall Masons. James Henderson (1845-1925) was an early local leader. He was born an enslaved person when his owner, Jake Henderson, brought him to Hannibal from Kentucky.

In this 1930 photograph, Masons from all over the state pose for a picture outside the twenty-one-room mansion built in 1906: the Prince Hall Grand Lodge Masonic Home at 4210 Market Street. Statewide chapters and even the highest-level grand masters were present, including locals Elmer Doolin (1889–1955), a World War I veteran, and Joseph Pelham (1848–1928), an 1897 Mason Grand Wizard. The occasion for this statewide event is unknown.

entrepreneurs, teachers, and school administrators. To empower, educate, and advocate for our own.

The Prince Hall Masons were the most prolific and included leaders from St. Louis and Kansas City. They had come together and built a state-sponsored, twenty-one-room nursing home on the outskirts of town as well as a meeting place at the Wedge in 1910. These were self-sustaining facilities, and families often provided food in exchange for the care of their aging relatives. The meeting place was razed in 1980 when the property was sold to the National Food Store. The old folks' home closed in 1966 and the latest owners are the Poage car dealership.

The United Brothers of Friendly (UBF) had four local temples. They also had an old folks' home on the outskirts of town, with very responsible caretakers on a self-sufficient farm, which included a huge garden, cattle, hogs, and chickens. The old UBF Home still exists as a private home.

These fraternal organizations have lost popularity, and our community is worse off for it.

Dressed to the nines, these women attend an early picnic at the Masonic Home.

CLUBS

Clubs were less abundant but just as committed to community service. The Fannie Griffin Arts Club, a chapter of the National Association of Colored Women Clubs (NACWC), was founded in 1971. Its founding members included Dorene Ambers, Grace Fouche, Lola Pearl Richardson, and Fannie Griffin. The group worked out of the former Holy Church at 1912 Settles Street. Their motto, "Lifting as We Climb," speaks to the mission of the organization.

Founded in 1896, The NACWAC was a social justice organization dedicated to Negro women's rights. One of its founders, Fannie A. Barrier Williams (1855–1944), had firsthand experience of life in Hannibal. After she graduated college in New York in 1870, she came to the town to teach at Douglass School. However, the racism, segregation, and violence she encountered here—which, having grown up in the Northeast, was new to her—is what led her to a life of activism. Ms. Barrier was a founding member of the NACWC; by her side was its cofounder, Harriet Tubman. Dr. Shelley Fisher Fishkin, a very generous patron of Jim's Journey, discovered and shared this nugget of information with me.

A convention of the Missouri State Association of Colored Women's Clubs, Inc. in the 1980s in Kansas City. In attendance are Dorene Ambers, Lola Pearl Richardson, and Ruth Thompson.

ELECTIONS

Harriett Hampton knew very well that she was making history on August 31, 1920, by becoming the first Black woman to vote in a local election here in Hannibal, Missouri. Harriet was born enslaved in 1863; she was brought with her parents from Tennessee. She worked her entire life as a domestic and was the wife of railroad worker William Hampton (1864–1919), who died before the infamous vote. She died in 1932 and is buried in Old Baptist Cemetery, likely lying alongside her enslavers.

Allen R. Bohon (1861–1945) also made local history as the first Black to ever serve on a jury in May 1941. Fast-forward sixty years to 1983 and we see the courageous Hiawatha Moore Crow (1904–1999) completing the paperwork to be on the April ballot for city council. In 1983, she became the first Black woman elected to local office—representing the Third Ward. An event so notable that she was featured in an edition of *Jet* magazine that year. She was reelected in 1987 and retired in 1993 after an unsuccessful reelection campaign. No Black person has been elected to Hannibal's city council since.

Melvin Dant (right) was a 1965 graduate of Hannibal High School. Despite receiving little support from his HHS counselor, he found his way to Hannibal LaGrange College. Going a step further, he became a student leader and was not your typical student. He wanted to make a difference and successfully ran for class officer. He was the first person of color in a student leadership position at this once segregated institution. It was in 1954 when Phillip Smith, a Douglass School valedictorian, was turned away from the institution, and it was still many years before a Black person was hired in a professional position in the Southern Baptist-run institution.

ELECT April 1993
HIAWATHA M. CROW

3rd Ward City Council

A Candidate For *All* the People

She wants Hannibal to be *Prosperous* and *Progressive*

Industrial development is one of my highest priorities. We need to provide jobs for our people. Unemployment is our number one problem.

We have to provide decent housing for our elderly and low-income people. Out city has a responsibility to take care of our needy and homeless.

We need to continue revitalizing down town. We should take pride in the historical areas of our city and do our best to restore them.

Our streets and sidewalks need to be rebuilt and/or repaired. having served as the 6th ward Councilwoman from 1987-1991, this project was high on my priority list.

My constant efforts to develop a sidewalk and repair ordinance was successful. Low cost loans are available for sidewalk repair.

We need city support for neighborhood organizations. They provide and important link to city government for residents and help develop pride and a desire to keep neighborhoods clean.

Educational Background:
Graduated Douglass High School
Bachelors from Culver Stockton College Canton, MO
Masters, Northeast Mo. State Univ. - Kirksville
Principal, Elementary School Administration

Previous employment after retirement from teaching:
- Former Coordinator, Hannibal Marion County In-Home Services for the Elderly
- Previously served from 1983 to 1991 Councilwoman of the 6th Ward
- Active in Church
- Active in Community

Paid for by Friends of Committee to Elect Hiawatha M. Crow, April Baldwin, Treasurer

This campaign ad was printed in a local newspaper. Hiawatha appears to be a sweet, unassuming woman, but this academically accomplished former teacher and administrator got things done. Like the first Black Democratic candidate, Shirley Chisolm, said, "a seat at the table."

In fact, the year Crow retired, the council voted to cut the number of council seats from twelve to six. As my dear cousin-sister, Betty Forte Scott, would have put it, "Now riddle me this": Why has no other person of color been elected to the Hannibal City Council?

Though Crow's election to public office was a historic victory for Hannibal's Black community, she was not the first to give it a try. Jesse Thurston (1887–1975), Arthur Green (1909–1969), and James Griggsby all ran unsuccessful campaigns for Hannibal City Council. Though they were all hardworking men and upstanding citizens of good character, they were not elected. Sue Fitzpatrick ran a campaign to be Hannibal's first Black mayor and lost to Mayor Roy Hark. As of 2013, there's been a Hark in that role ever since. It's debatable how good that has been for Hannibal.

ACTIVISTS AND INFLUENCERS

The NAACP began in 1909, when, following years of racial injustice and violence, a group of white liberals and African American leaders (including W. E. B. Du Bois, Ida B. Wells-Barnett, and Mary Church Terrell) came together. The nation's largest and most widely recognized civil rights organization was born.

Some years later, in 1925, the first local chapter of the NAACP was formed by president James T. Brown, and community leaders gathered to work on behalf of all citizens. They worked hand in hand with the Douglass PTA to affect change in the education system. They also fought for jobs and worked to combat discrimination. Past Hannibal NAACP presidents include C. A. Hopkins, J. T. Brown, Arthur (Ted) Green, William Sephus, Walter Sutton, James Griggsby, Rev. Silas Johnson, Rev. David Meeker, Rev. Jewell Jones, William Mallory, and Annie Dixon. The group has since been phased out.

Hannibal's NAACP chapter marching to honor Dr. Martin Luther King Jr. in 1985. More than one hundred marchers walked from the Wedge to the grounds of Douglass School and the current home of Willow Street Christian Church where a commemoration was held.

In the summer of 2020, hundreds of local protesters, Black and white, marched to take a stance on racial justice through the Black Lives Matter movement. This was part of a worldwide protest against the horrific murder of George Perry Floyd Jr. (October 14, 1973–May 25, 2020) by a police officer in Minneapolis, Minnesota. We were even able to convince the local Democratic Club to purchase a billboard that stood for months, reminding all driving near the Highway 61 and Market Street intersection that BLACK LIVES MATTER.

HANNIBAL'S FEARLESS ICE CREAM MAN

It takes a special kind of person to maneuver a small motor-powered vehicle around our Mississippi River town with the heat and the hills.

"It was a lot like driving a riding lawn mower up and down Hannibal's hills," recalled Osceola Edward Gibson, or Oscie (pronounced "O. C.") for short. "Definitely not an easy job on one of Hannibal's humid ninety-degree days." But he had the stamina to get it done.

With his ice cream cart, Oscie wasn't just challenged by Hannibal's hilly streets or hot days. It's 1963, before the Civil Rights Act and about six years after Hannibal's schools were integrated. A sixteen-year-old Black kid is riding all over town, beckoning kids—Black and white, in both rich and poor neighborhoods—to purchase an ice cream treat. An act of courage during tumultuous times.

"I don't recall being afraid," Oscie says about going into white neighborhoods. "But I was very cautious. It all depended on how that first street went. If it went well, I would proceed to the next one. Now there were well-known racially hostile neighborhoods that I steered clear of because of past experiences, including the South Side and Oakwood. But for the most part, I did not have any trouble at all." Black families, teachers, administrators, and stakeholders lived in many welcoming neighborhoods.

Stevie Letcher joins a protest in Hannibal in 1968. That year, local KKK members invited segregationist George Wallace to speak in Hannibal during his presidential campaign. More than two thousand of our neighbors showed up to hear him speak, but we made sure they heard our protests above his speech. Black students, clergy, residents, and community leaders ran George Wallace out of Hannibal that day. It was Friday afternoon, and there was no parade that Saturday morning as planned. Credit: Associated Press.

You could hear the steady cadence of Oscie's wagon bell ringing out from blocks away, giving kids plenty of time to go and "beg" for nickels and dimes to make a purchase. What an awesome job for a kid like Oscie, who is as personable, kind, and generous now as he was then. In fact, one of his fondest memories of his time as Hannibal's ice cream man was on those days he could give away crushed or broken ice cream treats to kids (oftentimes his own cousins) in the poorer neighborhoods.

"My favorite—and it continues to be—was the Ice Cream Bar," Oscie said of his lifelong sweet tooth. "The Dreamsicle would be next."

Hannibal was Oscie's boyhood home. He grew up here with his parents (Russell and Marie), two brothers (Howard and David), and two sisters (Elsie and Rhoda) for the first eighteen years of his life. His family had lived in Hannibal for generations, many in the home on Broadway where he and his siblings grew up. His ancestors included some of the town's local enslaved citizens.

Oscie started the seventh grade at the brand-new, integrated junior high school. Black and white students together for the first time. In high school, his driving instructor, Coach Jay Willows, got to know the kind of guy Oscie was and knighted him as Hannibal's ice cream man. After Oscie received his driver's license, Willows offered him and a fellow classmate a job driving one of his two newly acquired motorized ice cream carts. Oscie ended up working two summers for Mr. Willows.

"The first person I remember calling me 'the Ice Cream Man' was Rhonda Hall," Oscie remembers. "She lived at the foot of Hill Street and was one of the first little kids that frequented my cart when I entered Douglasville."

Oscie smiles, remembering how Jay Willows was the first adult to let him drive a car; even his father hadn't let him do that yet. "The cart on my route broke down," Oscie recalled, "and when Mr. Willows arrived to check on it, he casually tossed me his car keys and sent me to a local garage for a part. This took me by surprise. I drove his family car all by myself. Jay was alright with me."

Oscie had come to know Coach Willows through church. The two Baptist congregations, Eighth and Center Streets Missionary Baptist Church and First Baptist—one Black and one white—attended an annual service at each other's congregation.

"I was surprised to see him there," Oscie said. "I remember his anointed voice. He sang 'Jerusalem' in such a powerful way that it has stuck with me to this day."

Jay Willows and his wife, Peggy, remained lifelong friends of Oscie's until Jay passed away in 2017. Oscie still calls Peggy Willows annually to wish her a happy birthday.

Oscie recently returned to Hannibal for his high school reunion, celebrating the year he and his classmates turned seventy-five. He got a chuckle when he accepted the invitation to play golf on the local country club's one-hundred-year-old greens. His memories of the place are not so fond, though. Family and friends had maintained the grounds and facilities, and they had cooked and served meals and drinks, but they were never welcome to join the club, never invited to enjoy a meal, swim in the pool, or play golf.

"I remembered it as segregated," Oscie said. "And very exclusive. It was once a rich, whites-only establishment. And I enjoyed my morning on the greens with people whose parents had maybe fought fiercely to exclude me."

Osceola Edward Gibson often tells people that God took him out of Hannibal, relocated him to Chicago, and blessed him to prosper. He left Hannibal at eighteen to serve four years in the US Navy, serving two tours of duty attached to the RVAH-13 Reconnaissance Attack Squadron in the Vietnam arena aboard the *USS Kitty Hawk* and the *USS America*. Using his military service benefits, he attended and graduated from the Loop Junior College and later graduated from Roosevelt University, Chicago Campus, with a bachelor's of science in business administration. He is a retired radio engineer (WLS Radio, Chicago), and he worked sixteen years in a security position for the State of Illinois' Juvenile Division. He is overcome with joy in his current role as Bishop Osceola Gibson, the pastor of Dixmoor Community Church in Dixmoor, Illinois. Bishop Osceola and his wife of almost fifty years, Martha, have a daughter, Stephanie Watkins, a son-in-law, Lael, and three beautiful grandchildren: Dana, Micah, and Nyah.

First anniversary

PYRFEECT will be celebrating the one-year anniversary of the PYRFEECT Steppers with an awards ceremony and banquet at 6 p.m. Sunday, Feb. 23, at the American Legion Hall, Highway MM, Hannibal. The public is invited to attend. PYRFEECTS' "Through the Eyes of a PRYFEECT Child" Black History observance will conclude Monday, Feb. 24. The tours will be available from 9 a.m. to noon Monday and may be scheduled by calling (573) 221-8399. Leave a message. (Courier-Post photo/Mary Tolivar)

Children celebrating the one-year anniversary of the PYRFEECT Steppers. In 1996, community leaders Marilyn Powell, Paula Holliday, Rev. Faye Vaughn, Marsha Mayfield, Gale Conley, Georgina Hawkins, and Margaretta Williams founded PYRFEECT—Parents and Youth Reach for Education Excellence and Cultural Togetherness. Just as its name suggests, the mission of the group was to better the lives of local children. A Hannibal celebration of Juneteenth grew out of this organization; the objective remains to teach self-awareness and Black pride.

The man with the banjo is Maceo Wilson, playing here with the 100 Negro Chorus, officially named the Levee Singers (spiritual singers), for the 1936 Zephyr Railroad Dedication.

Chapter 9

WE SUNG! WE DANCED! WE LOVED!

Despite living under Jim Crow in Hannibal, we found joy—often it was music.

When it came to music, we sang in choruses, played in bands—school and otherwise—participated in plays, and joined church choirs. We were on the radio, TV, and in films all over the country. Our community has been blessed with a tremendous amount of talent. Albert Riding was a well-known musician. Sonny Gibson was in the Harlem Nights. Dora Kyer was a member of the Fisk Jubilee Singers at Fisk University. Robert Townsend was one of the singers in the Five Heartbeats.

Antonio Maceo Wilson (1896–1974) was married to a woman named Sylvia Cotton. He was an accomplished community leader—World War I veteran, a Mason, and the founder of the Colored American Legion Post #155. He was also a pianist who traveled the Midwest with his orchestra, the Virginia Ravens, a ten-piece band. The group broke up in 1929, and in the fifties, when he retired from the road, Wilson worked as a music teacher. Kids and adults were invited to his little yellow house on Olive

Street. I'm always meeting someone who was a student of Mr. Wilson—from J. T. Brown to Wells Pettibone to Gregg Andrews—and many of them are still performing more than fifty years after his death. He was not just a musician but also a civic-minded man who contributed much to the community.

The Levee Singers were an early Hannibal local singing group—church choirs were our earliest. In 1936, the Levee Singers performed in a play, *Mark Twain's First One Hundred Years*, the story of Sam Clemens as a riverboat pilot. Jim's Journey has a copy of the program from this 1920 play, presented on the Hannibal High Athletic Field. Because Hannibal was hyper-segregated, Black people were in the play but not welcome to be in the audience. It was a play written for Hannibal's Centennial Celebration, the most well-attended event of the year. There were over 1,100 participants. Most of the cast were white women and girls, though about one hundred African Americans also appeared on stage—mainly as spiritual singers in episode four. Three other Coloreds performed as "two Servants (Colored)" and another as a "Negro Mammy" in episode two.

If you watched films or listened to the radio in the 1940s, you may have seen Korla Pandit, aka John Roland Redd. He was a Douglass School student when his father, Rev. Ernest Redd, pastored at Eighth and Center Streets Missionary Baptist Church. The family moved to Hannibal in 1920 and lived here for nine years before returning to Columbia. Identified as a musical protégé, he often performed with adult choirs and in local plays. In the 1940s, John moved to Los Angeles and adopted the persona of Korla Pandit, pretending to be South Asian. He was the star of the first all-music program on television. His identity was finally revealed in 2000, after his death.

A local band performing at the Girard Street American Legion: Big Richard Simon is on the drums, and the other players include Edward Gibson, Tink Buckner, Jerry Jones, and Robert "Sonny" Gibson, and an unidentified man on bass.

Unidentified Blacks cutting up at the Legion, where they could hear nonstop R&B music from a local band or the jukebox.

The Mighty Men of Song performing for an audience in the Douglass School auditorium.

The Ladies Community Chorus at Eighth and Center Streets Missionary Baptist Church in the 1940s.

A girls' night out in the late 1950s. Gracie Fouche, center, standing with Alice Dixon, Velma Clark, Hiawatha Crow, and two unidentified women.

An evening out partying. MaryLou Nearing (second from the left) with friends.

A community gathering, I can identify James "Pick" Riding (left, standing) and Mr. James Crow (right, sitting). Could have been the Cement Plant Employee Picnic—definitely segregated—a different time and place.

SONNY'S CARS

Sonny Fitzpatrick, a seventy-something-year-old Black man, is unique for many reasons. Some may even call him a renaissance man—he's a husband, father, grandfather, entrepreneur, veteran, and a passionate collector of classic cars, into which he has invested a lot of time and money.

When given an opportunity to talk about Hannibal, he took the opportunity to talk about his love for cars. It's a story about how, despite the odds stacked against him, he achieved an impressive level of success. Sonny is an extraordinary man in many ways. His path to success can only be attributed to hard work and determination.

He was born in 1944 and raised by his grandmother in a modest little house on Settles Street, right next to the creek. He married a "Quincy girl," Sue Fonza more than fifty years ago.

Today, the Fitzpatricks live in a lovely home far from "the Black area," and Sonny's basement is filled with photographs of his more than fifteen salvaged and rebuilt cars. There is also a huge collection of die-cast cars no larger than the palm of my hand. I lost count at two hundred. They are beautiful, and he tells me they're built from zinc alloy and were carefully modeled after real-life designs produced by automobile manufacturers. "This is an exact replica of the 1967 Chevy Impala owned by Billy Cotton," he said. "Even the color [it's a pale yellow] matches his car exactly."

I go into another room, and there are more framed photographs of cars—this time, they are Corvettes.

With a twinkle in his eye, Sonny shared a photo of the first and last Corvette he purchased from Poage Auto, a C4.

"Yep, I had a cashier's check from my bank," he remembered. "Poage was fortunate to have the car, and I was fortunate to get it. I heard that they had received a C5, I approached them to purchase it. When they refused to sell me the C5, which they received because of my C4 purchase, I never bought another vehicle from them."

A proud member of the legendary Chevrolet Corvette Series Club (C-club), which began in the 1980s, Sonny has owned more of them than anyone else in Hannibal. If I have it right, he's owned nine Corvettes. On special occasions, his wife, Sue, drives designated dignitaries in their 2015 navy-blue Corvette convertible. Missouri State Senator Barbara Washington rode in it in Hannibal's 2022 Juneteenth parade.

Sonny belongs to two car clubs, the local Loafers Car Club and the Just Us Street Rod Club out of St. Louis, an all-Black club of vintage car owners. It's a great source of pride when he joins them in Quincy (across the river) for the Tin Dusters event.

His passion for cars likely began when he was a toddler rolling one from one end of the living room to the other. He was only fifteen years old when he purchased his first car, a 1949 Ford; he financed it at seven-dollars per week, which he earned while working as a farmhand for Dr. Miller. He got it even before he was licensed to drive. This car was followed by a '52 Mercury and '55 Ford, and those were followed by a new car or truck every couple years.

The much younger Sonny had a reputation for being a fast driver, and I had to ask if he'd ever been in an accident. "The only car accident I've ever had was when I ran over one of Freddy LaJoy's ducks," he recalled. "The whole neighborhood could hear him yelling at me. He said I owed him three dollars for it. My neighbor and friend, Miss Lola Pearl Richardson, gave me the three dollars to pay him, insisting that I come home with the duck. I knocked on Freddy's door for the exchange, only to find out that in that ten-minute absence, Freddy had the duck in a pot on the stove."

Sonny and his wife, Sue, have four sons, twelve grandchildren, and four great-grandchildren. He treasured his education at Douglass School as well as the ten years he spent in the Army, when he volunteered and served in Vietnam, Germany, and Korea. He sold his bar, Fitz's, about six years ago and is now retired, but he still maintains a shop to rebuild classic cars.

Kevin McLeod (1957-2019) one of the cutest kids in Hannibal. Looks like he's about two years old and all dressed up for church. Kevin was born in 1957. Years ago, he spent the morning hunting turkeys on our farm and was having a cup of coffee in our kitchen. I had to ask about his experience growing up biracial. His parents, Wanda McLeod Ely (1938-2019) and Joseph McAfee Ely (1926-2003), were an interracial couple forbidden to marry in Missouri. In the sixties, Missouri was one of sixteen states that did not allow interracial marriage. They crossed the river on June 25, 1965, to marry in Quincy, Illinois. The law existed until the 1967 *Loving vs. Virginia* ruling from the United States Supreme Court struck the prohibition down. Kevin said it was tough and that his mom's folks had a very hard time accepting it. He told me his biggest regret was the knowledge that he was never allowed to call his father "Dad" in public. It was dangerous.

Virginia Howard Collier (1934–1976) and husband James Collier (1934–2019). What a beautiful smile on Virginia's face. Forty-two-year-old Virginia was gone way too soon when she passed in 1976. Sickle cell disease is an inherited red-blood-cell disorder that predominantly affects Black people, and, over time, its symptoms include infections and episodes of intense pain. Virginia's surviving children, Arlene, Donna, and Duane (baby sister Romana died as an infant), tell a lovely story of a lifetime of memories of a loving mother who made them the center of her life, with family and friends always around to pitch in if necessary. But they also have memories of a mother who was in and out of the hospital, struggling to stay alive. Her wish was to "live to see her children grow up." She did. They also recalled how their father, James Collier, took frequent trips to the hospital to donate blood for her transfusions. Those transfusions lessened Virginia's pain and prevented other complications. This love likely prolonged her life.

Left: Patricia Smith Ford shares a bite of wedding cake with her brand-new husband, James Ford, on March 5, 1966. Their wedding took place at Patricia's Hill Street home. Parents Sam Smith (1900–1983) and Barbara Douglas Smith (1898–1970), family, and friends were looking on.

Chapter 10

RUN, JUMP, DRIBBLE, THROW

George Coleman Poage was born in Hannibal in 1880 to formerly enslaved parents, Anna Coleman Poage and James Poage. A former employer of James had made a move to Wisconsin, and his parents then made the decision to follow them—better the devil you know—and La Crosse, Wisconsin, provided more opportunities. George and his sister Nellie both graduated from LaCrosse High School, and he ranked second in the class. As a teen, he excelled both in academics and athletics. He also was the first African American to graduate from the school. Poage received his high school diploma in 1899 and his BS from the University of Wisconsin in 1903. Recruited by a local athletics club, George Poage ran track in the 1904 St. Louis Olympic Games and was the first African American to ever win an Olympic medal. He stayed in St. Louis, where he landed a teaching job at Sumner High. He eventually ended up in Chicago, working thirty years for the US Post Office until his 1962 death. Imagine sorting mail next to an Olympic medal winner. Credit: University of Wisconsin-LaCrosse, Murphy Library.

It's hard to know just how many athletic careers were cut short in Hannibal. The postwar years were the era of the integration of America's professional sports, when Jackie Robinson, Althea Gibson, Bill Willis, and others became household names.

Local athletes all tell the same story of being robbed of records, victories, or opportunities because of the color of their skin. But even under Jim Crow, many in the community found athletic success. And, in recent years, some have even become coaches. Members of our community went as far as the NFL and even to the Olympics.

In 2018, Hannibal's Black History Month celebration was held at the Hannibal Admiral Coontz Armory, a WPA project built in 1939 that the Hannibal Parks and Recreation Department manages. It has indoor basketball courts and a walking track, and the Parks and Recreation Department hosts field trips, events, senior dances, and pickleball games. The concrete walls of the building are pretty blank except for an enlarged poster acknowledging our most accomplished local athletes—Hannibal's Wall of Fame. On that wall, there is one solitary name of a Black man—Joe Miller.

Big Richard Simon (1906–1983) dreamt of becoming a professional boxer. While he appears more than ready to become a professional lightweight, he became a mechanic to support his family.

More often than not, Joe has been "the only one in the room." He was in the first integrated Hannibal High School graduating class in 1957. "Yes," he recalled, "I was an athlete at Douglass and Hannibal High. Me and Lester Black also started for the white high school basketball team."

He was also a fast-pitch softball player and manager for more than twenty years with Milt's Club.

"I started out playing first base, then pitched for about seven years and retired as player and manager," Joe said. "We played in the district playoffs for fourteen years. I retired from the game in 1982."

Miller has many accomplishments and has broken many barriers in his short eighty-five years. His life has seen him go from segregated Douglass School to the Hannibal Public School Board (two terms from 1975 to 1981), the YMCA Board, the FolkLife Festival (as a vendor for thirty years), a member of the Evening Kiwanis Club, and as a successful entrepreneur.

Joe was very fortunate to be there when Douglass School was in its heyday. He is a lifetime member of Disciples of Christ Christian Church and was there many years later when Raymond Brown had the foresight to purchase it for Second Christian Church. He was there in 1961, when the church moved in, and he was there when the old school was torn down in 1980. He has been a fixture at Willow Street Christian and was there when the new church was built in 1996. Mr. Miller was active in the NAACP, a testament to his commitment to family and community service.

"We had church in the Douglass auditorium which held so many memories," he said. "For a number of years, we sponsored a Summer Playground Program, led by Coach Oscar Estill on the grounds; kids walked a couple of miles from Douglasville to participate. Here it is, 2022, and we still use the little building [built in 1945] where Mr. Powers taught me mechanical drawing and woodworking and Mrs. Hobbs taught sewing and cooking. In later years, Mrs. McElroy even held a Head Start program here. I remember this because we enrolled our five-year-old, Michael—he was put out for being too smart for the class." Joe smiled broadly when he shared this.

Joe married his high school sweetheart, Gloria "Jane" Williams Miller (1937–2020), and they were together for sixty-four years. They had six children, twelve grandchildren, and nineteen great-grandchildren. He retired in 2015 as vice president of American Prearranged Services, Inc.

Larry "Bucky" Ely (1945–1978). At the time this photograph was taken, Ely was 6'5" and 315 pounds, the largest high school football player in the state. Hannibal, like the rest of Missouri, is a football town. After Hannibal High School integrated in 1955, Douglass School didn't have a football team, so this was the first time Bucky had put on a football helmet. Black athletes like Bucky often carried their teams to record-breaking victory, even though they were treated with disrespect in those early years of integration. Bucky was part of the first integrated Hannibal Public School graduating class of 1956. Many believe that Bucky would have been an athletic powerhouse at both the college and professional level had it not been for racial discrimination limiting his opportunities.

—Courier Post Photo

Basketball is a major sport after the close of the football season.
Row one: Gary McCarty, Dick Schutze, Paul Brown, David Pilcher, and Joe Miller.
Row two: Coach Jim Ballinger, Lester Black, Houston Barber, Dick Siemon, Kent Brown, Jim Way, Ben Tucker, Harlie Love, and Mr. Darold Davis, assistant coach.

Hannibal's first integrated Pirates basketball team, 1955. Hannibal High School first integrated its basketball team in 1955–1956. The Black players on the team were Lester Black, Alonzo Barber, and Joe Miller. "I started," Joe remembered. "The coach told us that he would have started all three Blacks, if he was not afraid of community backlash." As a Douglass Eagle the previous year, the three young men had been all-conference district champions.

Merrill Maurice "Mo" Forte (1947–2021), pictured here in his role as receiving coach for the Denver Broncos. Maurice had a long career in sports. He was born in Hannibal to Rosalee and Merrill Forte with two older sisters, Betty and Priscilla. Mo had attended Douglass School, he integrated the new Junior High School, and he graduated from Hannibal High School in 1965. He was recruited to play football at the University of Minnesota, where he became a standout athlete. After college, he went on to play a year as a receiving back for the St. Louis Cardinals (NFL) before becoming a receiving coach for the Denver Broncos, followed by the Detroit Lions. Mo ended his coaching career with several HBCUs. He recently passed away at his home in Pine Bluff, Arkansas, after a long and illustrious college and professional career.

Our own Ruby Bridges, Thersia Bright Cavil. Her father, Louis Bright (1923–2016), enrolled her in the first grade at the all-white neighborhood school, Central. They lived on Hill Street. It was 1955, long before Douglass Elementary closed (1959). You can probably tell by her expression that she wasn't real happy, and she was also not to be toyed with. Thersia is still one of my best friends. She's done well for herself, living in suburban Chicago.

Chapter 11

INTEGRATION HAPPENS

I was born in 1949 in Hannibal and grew up in the Midwest as a Black woman, a minority surrounded by whites. Hannibal has a population of about seventeen thousand people; it's 82.6 percent white and 11.8 percent Black. It will come as no surprise that Hannibal's highest Black population was just after Emancipation, when we made up 25 percent of the people who lived here. This changed as I married and lived in more urban communities of young Black professionals until my return to my hometown, Hannibal.

In those years not so long ago, I often felt like the self-styled fly in the buttermilk. Even if you've never heard that expression, you can imagine what it may feel like. Our white neighbors were barely aware of our existence until 1955, when things changed forever—or did they? Even after the end of legal segregation, it was still a major feat for a Black family to get a bank loan or move into one of the "better" (all-white) neighborhoods. And for many years, we continued to struggle like the fly in the buttermilk. As a teenager, I learned to survive. And I witnessed many in the community who have had an opportunity to "put away their mop."

Patricia Jackson (Smith) Ford is an awesome storyteller and wanted to talk about the three most supportive men in her life, with its somewhat tragic beginning. She lost both parents by the time she was fourteen months old. Tuberculosis took her mother, Matilda Givens Jackson, and her father, Lester Jackson. Both of them died at the Mt. Vernon State Sanitorium. Matilda was twenty-six and Lester was thirty. They left behind six children: Gerald, William, Floweree, Jacklyn, Loretta, and Patricia. Patricia learned later of the segregated Quonset hut-like barracks where Negroes were "cared for" at Mt. Vernon, where the death rate from tuberculosis was about three times greater than the rate for white people. Knowing her fate, Patricia's mother began looking for homes for her children, and they were all placed in loving homes before she died.

Samuel Henry Smith (1900–1982) and Barbara Smith (1898–1970) were chosen to raise Patricia, Matilda, and Lester's littlest angel. They were perfect for baby Pat. They lived in a modest, two-bedroom home at the foot of Hill Street. Sam worked for Charlie Davis as a horse trainer; Davis owned a stable on the outskirts of Hannibal. They were a loving family; their daughter Ada had left home by the time Pat arrived. While Pat was an infant when she arrived, they encouraged her to know and love her birth siblings. Of course, Patricia loved Mother (Barbara Smith), but Daddy (Samuel Henry Smith) was special to her. He came to her rescue on more than one occasion, he protected her, he even purchased her first prom dress (even though they couldn't afford it), and he taught her love and kindness. Mother was never very healthy, and when her crippling rheumatoid arthritis took a grip on her, Sam taught Patricia to help cook and care for her (and her little sister, Sammy) with compassion. Baby Sammy, Mother Barbara's granddaughter, came to live with them when Patricia was eleven years old. Sam loved and cared for his ailing wife in their home until she died. She was seventy-one.

Barbara and Sam also taught her to stand up against the power structure and white privilege.

"I remember my dad's employer, Mother's contemporary, admonishing her for not calling him Mister. She stood up to him: 'Charlie, I beat your ass when we were kids and can call you what I want.'"

When Patricia confronted her dad about why he allowed white people to say things like "son and boy," his response was, "I do this so we can eat."

"He was a gentle soul, very soft-spoken. I can remember him spanking me only one time and," as Patricia remembered it, "I was being a smart aleck and it was only a tap."

There was no annual yearbook to document Hannibal's first integrated classes. This May 1956 *Black and Red* school newspaper replaced it. It was published by the high school journalism class.

1955  1956

the
BLACK
and
RED

"It was 1955, schools were legally integrated. I was going into the seventh grade. Dad walked me the three blocks to the all-white Central school. We walked into the principal's office, and he announced that I would be coming here. My bedridden mother needed me to check in with her every day at lunch. It meant that I had to leave Douglass and all my Black friends and teachers, but I knew it was best. I showed up that September and saw all those white people. My heart broke all over."

That same employer, Charlie Davis, even tried to interfere with this act of courage. "I remember the phone call and hearing Daddy say, 'You take care of your child and I'll take care of mine.' It could have meant losing his job, but I guess Dad thought it was worth it."

Another testament to Samuel and Barbara Smith's kindness is the "found baby story," an event that happened before Patricia was born. It was in the late 1930s, and the family was leaving church when Mother heard the cry of a kitten coming from a trash can. Upon closer inspection, they discovered not a kitten but a baby boy abandoned and wrapped in newspapers. It was a time when Blacks were hesitant to involve the authorities—no police, no hospital. Sam supported Barbara's decision, and they added the child to the family. Sadly, the infant lived only a few months. Little Jessie died on August 2, 1938.

"Another awesome man who came to my rescue was my [birth] mother's oldest brother, William Givens (1922–2022)," Patricia recalled. "His job seemed to be to keep Mama's kids together and her memory alive. Every holiday, he traveled the countryside, gathering all six of us up to go to Vandalia for a visit with our grandfather, Floweree Givens."

Rev. Floweree Givens was a widower after his wife, Lulu, passed in 1939. He had also lost two daughters, Lorene (a mother of four) and Matilda. He now felt responsible for the ten orphaned grandchildren. "He gave and gave and gave," Patricia recalled. "He offered to adopt these grandchildren from his two deceased daughters, but everyone knew it was not best for us." Born in 1890, Rev. Givens died in 1965. "He was a strong influential man, taught all of us right from wrong." The grandchildren he helped to care for were pretty much grown and had begun to have children of their own. Patricia married another hometown kid, James Ford. His career took them to the St. Louis area and finally to Minnesota, where they raised three children, and they have several grandchildren and great-grandchildren.

Overruling the "separate but equal" principle set forth in the 1896 *Plessy v. Ferguson* case, the *Brown v. Board of Education of Topeka* case (Linda Brown died only in 2018) was a landmark decision by the US Supreme Court. The reality of separate but equal had not worked; it had to be remedied. Racial segregation in public schools was now unconstitutional, even if the segregated schools were otherwise equal in quality.

To my surprise, Hannibal was quick to respond. Douglass High School closed, and in September of 1955, grades ten through twelve integrated Hannibal High School.

Image from the 1955 yearbook—this is the Hannibal High School staff there to welcome our Douglass students.

The lone Black student council member is Clyde Wells, son of the former Douglass School principal.

Image of first HHS integrated band, the most integrated school activity. Douglass School was recognized as the highest achieving band in the state. Improved resources and new instruments only made them better.

Photograph taken from the 1970 Hannibal High School yearbook; the caption describes them as a cheerful group of students attending a pep club party. What I see is a group of Black girls creating their own party away from the larger pep club. Connie Hamilton and Toni Davis Rose are in the first row, and Jaque Brown-Williams, Debra Adams, and Bertha Reese are in the far back row.

Just as folks asked then and again today—"Why are all the Black kids sitting together in the cafeteria?"—I venture to guess that it continues to happen in most gatherings where folks are given a choice, despite the diversity of today. One reason folks from similar racial backgrounds gather is that connecting with peers who have similar experiences as your own serves as a buffer, offering some perception of safety, dignity, and acceptance. It can also be a way of affirming your identity, your value.

Rev. Silas Johnson was the first Black Hannibal public school teacher hired without Douglass School ties. He taught American history at Hannibal High School from 1970 to 1972. Just as he appears here, he was a very thorough historian and taught American history with passion. He passed away suddenly of a massive heart attack, leaving his students, his family, and his congregation to mourn him. Johnson pastored at Helping Hand Baptist Church.

Generations of Black people in Hannibal have had to navigate Missouri's virulent racism. We encountered barriers big and small at every turn but found ways to resist. Our community's contributions and accomplishments for the most part have been overlooked and consequently omitted from Hannibal's mainstream historical narrative. We hope to fill that void. It isn't about rewriting history; the objective is to expand your knowledge of local history. It's a story of progress in pictures.

About the Author

G. Faye Dant is the founder and director of Jim's Journey: The Huck Finn Freedom Center, a local Black history museum. She grew up in Douglasville in Hannibal, one of the oldest African American communities west of the Mississippi River. She is a fifth-generation descendant of enslaved Missourians and Civil War veterans. She left Hannibal in 1971 and did not return to Missouri to live until 2011. She married another local, Joel Dant, a sixth-generation Missourian. They have three adult children and three grandchildren. Faye was educated locally but received her bachelor's degree from Oakland University in Rochester, Michigan. After marrying, she went on to receive her master's degree from the University of Michigan. She and Joel lived in Michigan, Minnesota, and, most recently, Illinois, before returning to Hannibal. She is now retired after a twenty-five-year career in human resources. As a community historian and the curator of the Jim's Journey Museum, Faye is compelled to tell these stories of Hannibal's ordinary and extraordinary Black community—they all get a place on the walls of Hannibal's newest museum. As she describes it, "In 2013, I introduced Jim's Journey: The Huck Finn Freedom Center, the only Black history museum in northeast Missouri. I set out to share Hannibal's Black history, to reclaim our story. We also tell the story of Samuel Clemens the humanitarian, and reclaim the story of Jim in *Adventures of Huckleberry Finn*, who has been referred to more than two hundred times as 'Nigger Jim' for decades. Through research, I learned of Daniel Quarles (1808–1880), the real-life person who inspired the fictional Jim. Jim's Journey is the only museum in the country to pay tribute to Daniel Quarles, as he and some of his children lived and died here in Hannibal. As a community, we no longer have to be ashamed of Jim."